"Passing my faith onto my kids and their own faith is my number-one p

book, Casey is like your gentle best friend who provides Biblical wisdom, encouragement, and practical ideas for creating a home that honors God and leaves a legacy of strong faith that will impact generations to come."

—Steph Thurling, Executive Director of Christian Parenting and co-author of *Raising Prayerful Kids*

"With the voice of a mentor and friend, Casey reminds us of who we are in Christ, encourages us on our mothering journey, and reminds us that we are never alone. *Her Children Arise* invites readers to join the larger community of faith-filled women across generations, melding the challenges we face today with the biblical wisdom of those mothers who came before and those who will come after us. *Her Children Arise* is the encouragement we all need in our mothering."

—Kendra Roehl, mom of 5, author of devotionals including, *The One Year Daily Acts of Gratitude Devotional* and co-creator of the online community The Ruth Experience

"*Her Children Arise* is full of hope and biblical encouragement for moms in the trenches. In these pages, Casey inspires modern mamas through the stories of faithful mothers from the Bible. This book is a gift to the Christian mother's soul."

—Molly DeFrank, mom of 6 and author of *Digital Detox: The Two-Week Tech Reset for Kids*

"Full of refreshing stories and engaging biblical insights, *Her Children Arise* is the perfect read for any mom. I found it thought-provoking and faith-deepening, while also making me smile and nod along with Casey's stories of motherhood."

—Christie Thomas, mom of 3 and award-winning author of multiple books for Christian families

"This book is a helping hand to any mom who longs to leave a legacy of faith but isn't sure where to start. Casey's wisdom and witty humor empower moms to make eternal investments in their children that are sure to impact generations to come."

> —Erin Greneaux, mom of 3 and author of *Sunday God Meets Monday Mom*

"*Her Children Arise* will remind you of God's love and faithfulness to mothers of Scripture and to you as a modern-day mom. It will inspire and equip you to pass on a spiritual legacy to your children. *Her Children Arise* is a blessing for every mom."

> —Andrea Fortenberry, mom of 2 and Host of The Perfectionist's Guide to Mothering Podcast

"In a world where our faith is being tested, what a beautiful reminder of how living out our faith for our family can impact an entire generation. *Her Children Arise – Passing a Legacy of Faith to the Next Generation*, is a beautiful story of how the author's great-grandmother's faith shaped who she is today. This book brings hope, inspiration, and encouragement for our own parenting journey. Each day presents testimonies, scripture, and tangible ways to share our faith with our children at home. Such a timely piece."

> —Trudy Lonesky, mom of 4 and author of best-selling books *Reclaim Her Heart* and *Confidently Crowned*

"In *Her Children Arise*, Casey combines her incredible talent as an artist and crafter of words to create a book that uplifts and inspires women in the midst of motherhood. The Christ-centered principles she instills through various mother figures in the Bible, as well as fun applications for the family, help cultivate the soil for a legacy of faith in our children. You will leave these pages with transformative lessons that linger in your mind and touch your heart."

> —Becky Beresford, mom of 3, author, speaker, coach, and Brave Women Series Host

HER CHILDREN ARISE

her children arise

PASSING A LEGACY OF FAITH
TO THE NEXT GENERATION

BY CASEY HILTY

LIKE EDEN PRESS

james, john leyson, & lena

Your legacy of faith began many generations ago.
Through you, God has answered your ancestors' prayers.
And mine.

CONTENTS

A NOTE FROM THE AUTHOR

Summers at White Bear Lake, Mamie would sit in the living room very early in the morning, a shawl around her and Bible on her knee. Who of my grandchildren will carry this on? Mama kept it up. I take the time for it after breakfast. I haven't always done this. It is one of the advantages of living in a retirement home, old and with leisure time. However, young people with children can find some time for a few minutes with the family to read a verse or two, pray, and thank God for all His care and love. When the children were little and we were at the lake cottage, we did just that every morning.

— Gay Ferrey Dellinger

An excerpt from my great-grandmother's memoirs

1983, the year I was born

I was nine years old when my family took a trip from New Orleans to Austin to celebrate my great-grandmother's one hundredth birthday. Her children, grandchildren, and great-grandchildren gathered around a banquet hall to share a meal. I squeaked out a simple no-frills or trills version of "Happy Birthday" on my half-size violin to the applause of my parents, aunts, uncles, grandmothers, and family members I met moments before. Grandma Gay was so proud. I wonder where her thoughts took her as she scanned the room and observed her legacy before her eyes. Not many people witness a full century of life on Earth.

In 1983, my grandfather transcribed handwritten and spoken accounts of her life for her children and grandchildren. A few years ago, my mom passed her memoir down to me. I was nearly finished writing the Bible study version of *Her Children Arise* when I came across the words above: *Who of my grandchildren will carry this on?*

The Word of God has outlived every generation before us since the beginning of time. Before the written account of the Word, there was the spoken Word. God's story has been passed from generation to generation. The Word of God could have been extinguished thousands of years ago if not for parents passing faith down to their children. The home is and has always been a mission field for parents to teach the heart of God and the gospel of Jesus Christ.

But the world we live in is noisier than ever. We praise productivity over stillness, and busyness over rest. Our Bibles collect dust as we reach for our phones. Meals are on the go as we run from football to dance to robotics to piano. The dinner table gathers more junk mail than prayers. Our brains are inundated with dates, times, logins, passwords, logistics, and our child's GPA, yet we don't take the time to learn Scripture. The world tries to replace

God's truth with societal standards. Parents are over-scheduled, overworked, and overwhelmed. We try to squeeze God into our day rather than giving Him sovereignty over our lives.

I don't know about you, but sometimes I lose sight of my most important mission.

How do we navigate life as a mom? How do we juggle all the things? Where is the manual for motherhood? Where's the video series on how to make sure our kids hear about and know the love of God? Here are my great-grandmother's recollections from the late 1890s and her advice to mothers:

> *Young people with children can find some time for a few minutes with the family to read a verse or two, pray, and thank God for all His care and love...we did just that every morning.*

Whether we have a long line of godly women in our family or we are the trailblazers, it is our privilege and duty to intentionally include Jesus in every facet of our lives. Legacies of faith can begin with us, be maintained by us, or can dissolve with us.

It's as simple and significant as my great-grandmother witnessed from her mother. Invite Jesus into your everyday moments.

There's more to learn from the mothers who came before us. Written accounts of moms in the Bible teach us about faith, obedience, trust, love, servanthood, forgiveness, and more. Their stories have spanned thousands of years, been shared from generation to generation for thousands more, have traveled thousands of miles, and were translated into hundreds of languages into these Holy pages that are now divinely accessible to us. All of these women fought for the future of their families.

Like we do.

God has a purpose and a message for you and me, but He desires so much more. He desires to see us come to know Him. If we build the altar for Him in our lives, our children and the people in our lives will be drawn to God's glory. They will want a piece of it and they, too, will want to fall in love with Him.

Then we your people, the sheep of your pasture, will praise you forever, from generation to generation we will proclaim your praise.
Psalm 79:13

We are about to embark on a journey of growth and transformation that will spread from generation to generation. As His praise flows from our lips and our love imitates His, as His peace fills our homes and our eyes are set on things above, as we walk in obedience to His will and teach our children the ways of the Lord, there will never be a doubt that we are blessed and called. Our children are our testimonies.

"Her children arise and call her blessed..." (from Proverbs 31:28)

describes a mother whose children rise up to know Jesus, a mother who has put Christ in the center of her heart and home and who has led her children to fall in love with Him. This job of ours is sacred.

They may not "arise" every *morning* to call us *#blessed*. (Hello, toddlers and teens.) But as they rise in age and maturity, they will know of their mother's relationship with Jesus. And many will desire that for themselves. Our greatest prayer is that they will choose to follow Him.

The mothers we will read about are considered heroes of faith. Their walks were far from perfect, but they chose God's Word over the world. Though they had many moments that were not Pinterest-worthy, their character was God-honoring. Jochebed, Hagar, the Shunammite woman, Tamar, Rahab, Ruth, Bathsheba, and Mary left a legacy of faith in their wake. My great-grandmother left one for me and instructed me to do the same for my kids. Imagine what will be birthed from our faithfulness to raise up disciples within the walls of our homes.

To pave the way for our children to know God and teach them what following Him looks like, this book will cover five steps for us to take on our own faith journeys.

Step 1: *Trust in the Lord.* First, we surrender ourselves to God as believers in Jesus Christ, His Son. We let Him have access to the control panel of our lives, in essence.

Step 2: *Seek Him first.* We then desire to grow in the Spirit to become more and more like Christ. Pursue Him daily through the highs, lows, and mundane parenting moments.

Step 3: *Follow Him.* To do this, we put God's commands into practice. We have an open invitation to follow Him, but it takes sacrifice and obedience to do so.

Step 4: *Live out your faith.* Mothers who live out faith model His love. As we grow in knowledge of Him we are better able to share about Him and teach His Word to our children.

Step 5: *Serve the Lord.* When we walk with God as we parent, we become mission-minded in our role as mothers. We share the responsibility of shepherding our child's heart with God.

After each chapter, I've incorporated easy-peasy ways for you to start a conversation about faith in your home. Most of these activities can be done with items found around your house, but if you don't have them in stock, don't shop—improvise!

Let's pray together: *Father God, we love You and we praise You as our Creator, Healer, Protector, and Father. Guide us as we raise our children to know and honor You. May they rise up to be warriors for Your kingdom, another generation bowing to worship You. May Your favor be upon us for a thousand generations. It is in Christ's name we pray. Amen.*

trust in the Lord

But blessed is the one who trusts in the Lord,
whose confidence is in him.
Jeremiah 17:7

CHAPTER 1

PINKY PROMISES

I promised my kids I would take them on a bike ride. The ominous sky turned darker with thick clouds racing overhead. Glancing at the time and the never-ending to-do list, I knew a bike ride wasn't going to happen. I'd made a rookie parenting mistake: letting the kids know the plans for tomorrow. Plans change and, well, Mom takes the blame.

I'm both a promise-maker and a promise-breaker. I'm also a promise-manipulator. I'll give my word to my children, fully intending to carry the plan out until it slips my mind or until something prevents me from doing so. Sometimes I never lock it in on the calendar and keep putting it off.

"Sure, we can get a treat after the doctor's visit." Then, we arrive home having completely forgotten to stop at the drive-thru. "We'll go to the park tomorrow." Then, it rains. "We can go play with our friends soon." And that's where the manipulation comes in because "soon" has no precise deadline. Words like *soon* let me off the hook for a while. *Maybe* gives me an out. It's the ultimate "I'm not making any promises and I can change my mind" word.

I placate. I use promises to keep my kids happy when they can't have their way at that moment. Even without using the word, my kids still take everything I say as if it's written in stone. They like to hold me to these promises and they never, ever forget.

Here's a fun fact that encourages this promise-breaker mama's heart: God never breaks His promises.

His divine power has given us everything we need for life and godliness through our knowledge of him who has called us by his own glory and goodness."
2 Peter 1:3

His pinky promise.

How blessed are we that God never breaks His promises, forgets them, or manipulates them? His promises have always been grander than anyone could dream. We see them play out over and over in the Bible. Many of God's promises unfold around a faithful mother.

In the beginning, or shortly thereafter in Genesis 12, Abram (Abraham) was promised he would be made into a great nation, and his offspring would yield generations upon generations of people.

By the time Abram was nearly 100 years old and his wife Sarai (Sarah) was 90, it seemed God was a promise-manipulator, much like those of us who trick our kids into believing a promise by saying "one day soon." It didn't seem possible to conceive a child that late in life. Spoiler alert: God did not break His promise.

Sarah gave birth to Isaac who fathered Jacob. Jacob fathered twelve sons (through several wives). From their offspring, seventy Israelites originally went into Egypt, escaping famine in the land of Canaan. Eventually, the number of descendants had grown so much that the "land was filled with them" (Exodus 1:7). The Israelite population grew exponentially over the course of two hundred years. Fast forward a bit and, following the rise of a new Pharaoh, the Israelites became enslaved by the Egyptians (Exodus 1).

I can only imagine the bewilderment of God's people when they were enslaved. *Where is the fulfillment God would turn us into a great nation? Surely that didn't mean enslavement!*

Despite their hardships, their population grew exponentially. The Egyptian king feared the rising numbers of his slave population. The strength of the Hebrew people threatened his power. Pharaoh increased the oppression of the slaves, but God continued to bless His people with children. In an effort to "tame" the out-of-control population growth of God's people, the king told the Hebrew midwives to kill all of the baby boys they delivered.

But the women answered to God, and not an Egyptian king.

So God was kind to the midwives and the people increased and became even more numerous. And because the midwives feared God, he gave them families of their own.
Exodus 1:20-21

This verse not only refers to the two midwives Shiphrah and Puah, mentioned in verse 15, but to all Hebrew midwives in Egypt. Because of their reverence of Him and to fulfill His promise to Abraham, these women, whose job it was to deliver babies, also received the blessing of fertile wombs. God's kingdom here on earth grew through these resilient and faithful midwives. Pharaoh reacted to the threat of losing power by attempting to cut off God's people.

Through different circumstances, we see this pattern later in the Bible. In the New Testament, King Herod feared the fulfillment of the prophecy of the birth of Christ.

For out of you will come a ruler who will be the shepherd of my people Israel.
Matthew 2:6

King Herod's response was to—sound familiar?—kill all the baby boys two and under. In Jesus's earthly father Joseph's dream, an angel of the Lord revealed Herod's plan to find and kill baby Jesus (Matthew 2:13). Another promise. And we, ever grateful, live on this side of its fulfillment. History had repeated itself nearly 1500 years later, but God, as always, was faithful. He never forgets a promise—not during the time of Pharaoh's rule, not in Jesus' day, and not now.

As God blessed His people in those ancient days, Pharaoh pushed harder. He extended the order for all Hebrews, not just midwives, to kill newborn boys.

Both Pharaoh (Old Testament) and King Herod (New Testament) had the same downfall: they didn't fear God, they feared God's plan. They attempted to interfere with His efforts. It's as if these rulers knew the power of our Almighty God, yet they desperately held out false hope they could defeat Him.

We do the same thing when we disobey God. We challenge His plan for us. We question how we fit into His story. We ask "why" and "why not?" We think our personal agendas are better and more significant than what God has in store for us.

This life—our existence—is all part of God's story. He has made promises and has fulfilled every one of them. He promised Abraham his family would become a great nation and the fulfillment of that promise is etched across the pages of the Bible. Genealogies in the Bible may at first seem like a tedious list of names, but they are a written record of God raining blessings upon His people.

God is the Sovereign Author. Our failed attempts to shift the direction of the story, like Pharaoh's, cannot thwart His plan. God's divine design always prevails, and His story overrides our feeble efforts to change it. As His followers, we can't mess it up if we try. And girl, do we try.

When my husband's company was laying off workers, he surprisingly received a job offer in a town nearly two hours away. We were confident God's hand orchestrated the timing of the offer because, in all likelihood, Bo would have been laid off that month.

But the start of the new job did not align with the sale of our house. For three months we lived in two separate cities as—during each showing of our home—I loaded the minivan with kids, ages three and one, along with diaper bags, toys, lunch boxes, and the dog.

On weekends we would make the four-hour round trip drive to house hunt. We immediately fell in love with our new, quaint little town nestled on the bayou with its picturesque Main Street. We found a house we liked across the street from an elementary school, a short walk from a park. It seemed perfect for our family. But we couldn't put an offer on it until ours sold.

A few weeks later, the price of the ideal house dropped and we held out hope it would be ours. We were not-so-patiently waiting for our house to go under contract. When it finally did, we celebrated and made plans to put an offer on the new home. But the contract on our old house fell through.

How quickly our faith faltered. We questioned God's provision for our family. We doubted the move, even though it felt right. He had clearly spoken to us. But as time went on, we wondered if we'd heard Him right. It was a hard season of waiting.

Finally, three months into our long-distance living, our house went under contract and the price of the new home dropped again. Had God kept us waiting for the perfect price? I immediately packed up the kids and picked up my mom to drive across the long basin bridge to put an offer on the house. I wanted my mom there to witness God's faithfulness. But His faithfulness took an unexpected turn.

Our realtor said, "Before we go see the house you love, let me show you one that just came on the market."

As soon as we walked into this new-to-market home, the presence of God seemed evident in my heart. I didn't love the house—the lingering smell of cigarette smoke, the horrible maroon floral wallpaper border dividing the white top half of the wall from the bottom maroon half—but God made it clear it was home. I felt it pulsating within me. Our *home*. I shared the sentiment with Bo whose grin turned into a nervous laugh. He felt it, too.

I was confused by this abrupt change. Although we knew it was right, we still asked our realtor to show us the other house one last time. We wanted double assurance we were hearing God correctly. He had spoken quietly in our hearts before, but now we asked for absolute clarity.

As we walked up the steps to the house our realtor had shown us several times before, we noticed a gap at the threshold. How had we missed that? The front porch had detached from the house. Inside, cracks zig-zagged up the walls and across the ceilings. The foundation was unstable. The home was not the perfect home we had thought.

The sellers attempted to hide the dilapidation. God planned for us to move to that bayou town, and He was faithful to provide a stable and safe home for our family. In the 10 years we lived there, it weathered hurricanes, floods, and a few awful paint choices. Even though we questioned His timing and His provision along the way, it was clear where He wanted us. Like Abram, like the Israelites, we learned to trust God in the waiting.

> *The Lord Almighty has sworn, "Surely, as I have planned, so it will be, and as I have purposed, so it will stand."*
> Isaiah 14:45

This is a promise that will never be broken. God's faithfulness withstands millennia and kings and wars and famine and death itself.

> *His divine power has given us everything we need for life and godliness through our knowledge of him who called us by his own glory and goodness. Through these he has given us his very great and precious promises, so that through them you may participate in the divine nature and escape the corruption in the world caused by evil desires.*
> 2 Peter 1:3-4

The growth of a nation started with a promise to a father that was carried out through a mother—Sarah, "mother of nations." One of their descendants would arise to free God's people from slavery and lead them to His promised land. That person was Moses. God put it on Moses' heart to write down his humble beginnings in what would become the book of Exodus, chapters one and two.

In Exodus, he included the role his mother played. Moses' mom had to trust God in the hardest circumstances. Her story of unwavering faith, as we will discover, is one that teaches us to trust God. It's another example of how God will not manipulate or break a promise. He is not secretive, yet He deliberately reveals His plans to us in His time and in His way. He places desires in our hearts that He promises to fulfill, but how often do we naively question how all the pieces fit together?

In some ways, it's like a home makeover show. The preparation and anticipation can make us doubt the designer's choices, but the big reveal will be extraordinary in the end. I've never been disappointed in the outcome. I keep watching the episode because I trust the designers to know what they're doing.

Trust. We keep hanging on because we know that what is revealed is going to be good. Trust is the foundation of faith. Even though God's faithfulness is woven into the spine of the Word, the hardest part of our faith journeys is learning to trust Him.

What does God's promise to Abram look like today? Through His Son, God's people have grown beyond the borders of Israel and throughout the world. We who obey God and follow Jesus Christ are the recipients of all the good things He has promised from the beginning. No takebacks.

> *No eye has seen,*
> *No ear has heard,*
> *No mind has conceived*
> *What God has prepared for those who love Him.*
> 1 Corinthians 2:9

FAITH AT HOME

CREATE A PRAYER SPACE

Designate a spot in your home as a place of prayer. It can be a closet, laundry room, or even a corner. As a family, spend time transforming that space into a sanctuary. It can be the place each family member goes to when they are feeling overwhelmed and need to spend some quiet time with God. Here are some ways to make that space special:

- Actively pray in this sanctuary—by yourself, with your husband, with your children, or as a family. Invite the Holy Spirit to dwell in this space. Worship and talk to God in this space.
- Line the walls with Scripture and art. It doesn't have to be pretty or even permanent.
- On the wall, post the names, birthdates, and salvation dates of everyone who lives in your home.
- Keep a chalkboard or dry-erase board handy so you can write a new verse each week for your family to memorize.

- Write your prayer requests on post-it notes and hang them. Designate an area (or basket, jar, or journal) for answered prayers, and praise God for His response.
- Use pillows, blankets, and subdued lighting such as a lamp or string of lights. Put a Bluetooth speaker there to play worship music.
- Keep Bibles, journals, colored pencils, paper, sticky notes, and musical instruments nearby for when creativity strikes.

Then people brought little children to Jesus for him to place his hands on them and pray for them.
Matthew 19:13

CHAPTER 2

HOW HE SEES US

My dad and I had a wonderful father-daughter relationship. He was strong, loving, smart, and creative. He loved to use his hands to build new things and repair old ones. His knowledge and skills seemed endless to me. He was a true jack-of-all-trades. I know how to change a tire, use power tools, and throw a football with a tight spiral—things all girls needed to know—because of him.

Dad was most content on a hammock in the woods or in a canoe on the bayou. He taught me to enjoy the peacefulness of nature. And to always leave places—such as campgrounds—cleaner than I found them. This is why I pick fallen items off store floors and place them back on the shelf. It's why I always return the grocery cart.

He was quite the trumpeter in his day. He introduced me to his love of music—rock and roll, blues, jazz, and his soft spot, classical.

From a young age, I wanted to play the violin. My dad would close his eyes as I practiced, hearing the notes bounce off the walls of our home. And though my music brought him joy, he respected my decision when I quit to be a cheerleader in high school. Though I'm sure it pained him to see me walk away, he still attended football games to watch me cheer on the sidelines...and to watch the game. Football was his favorite sport.

I went to Louisiana State University because he raised me to be a Tigers fan. He bought me a guitar. He secured a loan to help me fulfill my dream of studying abroad in Spain and took me to the airport to send his oldest daughter on a grand adventure...alone.

I only brought one boy home to meet my dad, and I ended up marrying that one. At their first encounter, Dad immediately put Bo to work in the flower bed—likely the most awkward meet-the-parents ever.

I graduated from college—something Dad had always dreamed of doing. He encouraged me to apply for a job as a teacher, even though the job sent me across the country to Los Angeles. Less than a year later, arm-in-arm, he walked me down the aisle. Six months later he passed away.

That was October. In November, a positive pregnancy test confirmed Bo and I were expecting our first baby.

For two years, my life was on a fast track: moving nearly 2,000 miles away, starting a career, juggling graduate school, getting married, losing my dad, pregnancy, having a baby, and then moving

back home to Louisiana to be a stay-at-home mom. Much of who I
am is because of who my dad was and who he raised me to be. And
yet, after I became a mom, I felt lost. I struggled to find my identity.

Who Are We, Anyway?

The first ten verses of Exodus 2 describe Moses' lineage, his
parents, and his birth. In the first half of the chapter, we learn about
his mother's courage, trust, unwavering faith, and sacrifice before
we even know her name.

Both Jews and Christians believe Moses is the author of the
Book of Exodus, yet here in the beginning of the book where his
mother plays a vital role, her name isn't even mentioned. We simply
know her as a Levite woman (Exodus 2:1-2) or Moses' birth mother.
She isn't introduced by name until chapter six.

"Moses' Mom." That's how she was known in the early pages of
Exodus. I find this convicting because I struggled with my identity
after becoming a mom. Yes, I knew this was part of God's plan for
me, and wanted it so badly, but I did not fully understand how much
this new role would change me. I did not realize it would take over
my former self and replace all of me with a new identity.

Even though I didn't want it to, I resented that I was no longer
Casey, but Mom. Leaving my job as a teacher to stay at home, I
traded in work clothes for sweatpants, showers for spit-up, and
lesson plans for the never-ending pile of laundry. I told myself I was

not cut out for motherhood.

I felt like one of those characters in crime shows who go into witness protection:

New Name: Mom

Job Title: Diaper Changer

Parameters: Currently under house arrest

I tried to hang on to whatever was part of my old self, stripping off my mommy "hat" at each solo grocery run or date night. I even broke down in tears when my husband playfully sang across the house, "Oh, Mommy!" for the first time. New house rule: only the kids could call me Mom.

For my first Mother's Day, Bo bought me Dr. Seuss books to read to my son and planned for the three of us to spend the day at the zoo.

Together.

At the time, I was angry with him, even though it was a sincerely thoughtful gesture. I wasn't in the right place in my identity. Give up a day of pampering to instead spend it with my family? The horror! Isn't Mother's Day my one day off? Isn't this when Mommy goes to the spa alone?

Three kids later, I have a stronger sense of my purpose and calling in life. Rooted more deeply in my faith, I can now laugh at my first year of motherhood. (Yes, this "who am I" moment lasted at least a year, if not longer). I've fully embraced motherhood, from messy bun to minivan. Ironically, I entered yet another identity crisis when my youngest started kindergarten and I no longer had babies to take care of during the day. Who am I besides "Mom"?

The exclusion of Moses' mother's name in the first few chapters of Exodus emphasizes how God uses ordinary people to do extraordinary things. From an ordinary woman and an ordinary man, God raised up a redeemer for His people. Names, titles, and accolades aren't important in the eyes of God. There is no need to mention her name yet because her character was known by God. He knows her name, just as He knows you and me by name.

Read the following verses below to learn how God sees you:

And the Lord said to Moses, "I will do the very thing you have asked, because I am pleased with you and I know you by name."
Exodus 33:17

But now this is what the Lord says—he who created you, O Jacob, he who formed you, O Israel: "Fear not, for I have redeemed you; I have summoned you by name; you are mine."
Isaiah 43:1

I am the good shepherd: I know my sheep and my sheep know me.
John 10:14

These verses remind us that we need no other identity than who we are in Christ. He does not call us by what we have accomplished or by our talents, our roles, or even our sins. He does not call us by our careers or genealogies. He calls us by our character, who we are in relationship to Him. That is our true name, our true identity.

The question was raised on a radio program, "Have you, the mother of your children whom you love more than you can even grasp, ever counted the number of hairs on your child's head? Have you ever even attempted it?"

God, who loves us to the moon and back, then circling Pluto a few times and then some more, knows and loves us so well he has memorized every single, minute detail of us from our IQ to our DNA to our quirks and what makes us tick.

When we come to know the Maker of heaven and earth, the great I *Am*, Yahweh, God Almighty, our identity does change. When our hearts grow to love and put our trust in our Father, how can we not experience that transformation?

The names of several people in the Bible changed as they grew in their relationship with God. Abram, which means "exalted father," became Abraham, "father of many." Sarai, meaning "my princess," became Sarah, "mother of nations." Jacob, "supplanter," became Israel, "he struggles with God." And Simon, whose name means "God has heard," became Peter, meaning "rock."

In Exodus 6:20, we finally learn Moses' mom's name in the

genealogy of Moses and his brother Aaron. *Jochebed.* "Jehovah is her glory."

Jochebed, pronounced *JOK-uh-bed*, was presumably a Hebrew midwife. God was kind to the midwives for their faith in Him (Exodus 1:20). Jochebed feared the Lord and believed in His promises. God blessed her not only with the gift of a family of her own, but with the exceptional children she birthed: Moses, Aaron, and Miriam.

Moses was appointed by God to lead His people out of Egypt. Aaron became the first High Priest of the Israelites, appointed by God as Moses' prophet. And Miriam was a prophetess and songstress, whose praises of God are forever inscribed in Exodus 15 after He led the Israelites safely through the Red Sea.

God has used Jochebed's story to teach me about identity. She is known and remembered for her faith. It was part of her culture and her strength. Her role as a mother to Moses was wholly dependent on her faith.

In today's culture, we value achievements and pride ourselves on success. If we try to find our identity in what we have accomplished in life, we may feel robbed of our identity when we become a mom. Whether you stay at home, work from home, or work outside the home, your accomplishments and achievements as a mother aren't listed on the world's scale of success.

Children change us. They not only call us by a different name than what we have been known by our whole lives, but our bodies change. Our shape, our hair, our menstrual cycle, our skin—children change our physical appearance. They change our relationships, our friendships, our marriage. Relationships pre-kids are never the same post-kids. I'm convinced having children changes our chemical balance.

My friend and I were talking about the anxieties we now feel when we hear "Mom" on repeat, kids arguing, or just loud play. A house in chaos can send our once-calm demeanors into a whirlwind. We crave peace—or our idea of peace, which we imagine looks like children playing quietly with a puzzle on the floor instead of running around the kitchen island in circles like wild banshees, the dog barking, and toys being thrown everywhere.

We think peace on the outside will control the chaos we feel on the inside when really, it's peace from God that begins inside of us, allowing us to deal with the chaos on the outside. If we don't have that, we snap. We become the mom we never thought we'd be. If our sole identity is "Mom," then when we have a moment of failure, we are quick to relabel ourselves as "bad mom."

After church, errands, meetings, and Girl Scouts, I came into the house and stopped in my tracks. What I saw sent me into a downward spiral. My husband was covered in mud as well as the dog, cat, and kids. I yelled at everyone. I quickly left the room and ran to my closet to cry, feeling like the world's worst mom. I hated what I was feeling and how I reacted. If all I am is a mom and I can't even do that right, then who am I?

My kids saw my despair. (Yes, they followed me to the closet. Alone time does not exist.) I sobbed and apologized to them. But my younger son, John Leyson, reached over and held a hand-made sign over my head that said, "World's best mom under this sign." Isn't it amazing how kids see us as God sees us?

That moment may not have been one for the scrapbook, but God looks at our whole selves and doesn't keep a tally of our bad mom moments. We need that reminder to see ourselves as God sees us.

So, who is Jochebed? What is her identity? We know her as a slave. We know her as a midwife, a Hebrew woman, and a mother. But the sole reason she is in the Bible is because of her unwavering faith. God sees His glory through her. Her story isn't a resume to show off her education, qualifications, and previous experience. It isn't an Instagram feed of a picture-perfect home and family. It's a testimonial showcasing her strengths and character. Her identity is in God. Her character as a mother who faithfully puts her trust in God sets her apart.

What did these Hebrew slaves have without their faith and family? Nothing. Are you willing to strip away the identities the world treasures in favor of the new creation Christ has made you? A woman of faith. Appointed by God to be a mother of your/His children. He has something big planned not just for you, but for your future generations that will glorify Him.

God sees us as His beautiful creations, but for the longest time I didn't like what motherhood did to my body, my emotions, or my peace. I learned what my husband sees in me is better than what I see in myself. What my kids see in me is better than what I see. And if my husband and children can see a better version of me, then how much more does my God—who created me, who knit me, who intricately designed me—see me and know who I am?

Jochebed didn't have superpowers, but she put her faith in a powerful God. He carried her from suffering to hope. Who needs any other name, any other identity, any other role than that which we are called by God? "Jehovah is her glory." God is her glory. We can find identity in Him and He will shape all the other roles in our lives.

God has blessed us with the role of motherhood, but does motherhood define us? Sure, we may dress the part, but is this role our identity? Being a mom occupies a lot of headspace and heart space, but it is not what makes us tick. If it was, then when we compare ourselves to other moms, it would challenge how we see ourselves. And when our kids leave our nest, we would, once again, become lost. When we mess up—because we all mess up—how would we see ourselves? But when we as moms find our fullest identity in Christ, the Holy Spirit shapes and molds the type of mother we become. He called us to this role so we can pour our faith into the generations that come after us. Raising our children to become children of God is our biggest purpose on earth.

God knows each of us by name. It's important to enter into a relationship with Him to know Him by name as well. Yahweh, the Lord God Almighty, goes by many different names: Creator, Maker, Peace, Light, Healer, Protector, Guide, Shepherd, Provider, Master, Lord, Everlasting, and more. He is all these things to us. As you come to know Him, He will reveal more of who He is.

Meditate over the following verses and secure them as truth in your heart. What do His words say about how He cares for you?

"Because he loves me," says the LORD, "I will rescue him;
I will protect him, for he acknowledges my name.
He will call upon me, and I will answer him;
I will be with him in trouble,
I will deliver him and honor him.
With long life will I satisfy him and show him my salvation."
Psalm 91:14-16

FAITH AT HOME
MICRO-ZOOM

Using your phone or camera, take close-up pictures of each of your child's external features. Zoom in on his/her eyelashes, freckles, elbow dimple, toenail, hair, knuckles, etc. Talk about how God can even see our cells, our bones, our hearts, our brains inside of us, and all our thoughts and actions, too. He has a micro, micro, micro-lens that captures the details that are invisible to us.

And even the very hairs on your head are all numbered.
Matthew 10:30

N I L E   R I V E R   M O M E N T S

My middle child inherited my husband's internal alarm clock. He wakes up between five and six o'clock every day. I sense his presence when he hovers over me, silently begging my eyes to open. When they do, he sometimes has a game in hand for us to play together. Other times he just wants me to know he is awake before he starts his day.

One time, I got to sleep in on a Saturday morning. Just once. It's a rare occasion for a mom. When my youngest, Lena, was a toddler, the sun was peeking through the blinds when she climbed on top of me. The clock read 7:34 a.m. Still not an ideal time for a night owl, but the additional shut-eye felt like a gift from heaven.

Baby Girl is the snuggly one. She crawled in bed with the dog and me—Daddy was already engaged in an early morning project of some kind—sucked on her finger, and stared at me while I closed my eyes for another few minutes.

Ah, the cozy life. A warm, pillow-top bed adorned with Egyptian cotton sheets and a pin-striped duvet cover. The word *duvet* sounds fancy with its French roots. A framed poster of Vincent van Gogh's *Starry Night* hangs on one wall next to my grandmother's antique armoire. The mid-century modern piece has been preserved and passed down to me. Wedding pictures and diplomas adorn the other walls. A chest full of blankets—more than any one family could ever need—sits at the edge of our bed.

The air conditioner rests at a comfortable 74 degrees. We drop it down to 71 at night so we don't sweat under our covers. Among the bigger marital discussions as of late: *should we paint the wall trim White Dove or Floral White?*

There is not a hint of similarity between my twenty-first century, middle-class home nestled along the coast of a free and prosperous country and the homes of the enslaved Israelites in Egypt.

Walking by Faith

Take a minute to consider a mother's heart during the Israelite's days of slavery in Egypt. Many baby boys did not survive, and mothers' broken hearts grieved. Some mothers were able to hold their babies in their arms. Others had theirs ripped from them. It was a frightening time for families, as if living in slavery wasn't enough.

I'm pretty sure I would be a basket case (Get it? Moses... basket?) carrying the baby for nine months, knowing his fate if the little one was a boy. It's not quite the same reaction you would get at a modern gender reveal with balloons, cupcakes, and streamers. Nine excruciatingly long months, teetering between faith and fear. Oh, the prayers that would pour out of my heart for a little girl, meaning my baby could *live*.

With what Jochebed faced, my desire to have a little girl after having two boys purely to ooh and ahh over bows, glitter, and all things pink sounds frivolous.

And she became pregnant and gave birth to a son. When she saw that he was a fine child, she hid him for three months.
Exodus 2:2

Other translations use the words goodly, beautiful, and special to describe baby Moses (Ex. 2:2). The first time I read that verse I thought, "Well, of course she thought that. Who doesn't think that about their babies?" But there's a reason these descriptors are present not just in the Old Testament, but also in the New Testament.

At that time Moses was born, and he was no ordinary child.
Acts 7:20

In other translations of the book of Acts, the phrases *a beautiful child in God's eyes/sight, lovely in the sight of God, exceedingly handsome, fair or lovely, dear to God, and wonderfully beautiful to God* are used. In South Louisiana, we would have all exclaimed, "cher bébé!" (pronounced *sha baebae*) which in Cajun French means "darling baby." God's hand was on this child from the beginning.

When my first son was born, he was an around-the-clock cluster eater. I barely slept because he was either eating or crying. Rarely sleeping. At the time, my husband and I were living in a tiny apartment in Los Angeles with neighbors on all sides. We didn't have an air conditioner, so we often left our windows open to allow the sea breeze to flow inside.

Our arrival home from the hospital was announced by our two a.m. feedings. And the three and four a.m. ones as well.

It is a miracle no one discovered baby Moses had been born. All infants cry, right? When I picture this scene, I visualize a community of Hebrews living in little multi-family huts nestled close together. I can't imagine the Egyptians giving the Israelites the luxury of sound-proof insulation that would prevent a baby inside from being heard on the outside.

This *fine, special, goodly* baby remained safe with his mother for three months. Jochebed was faithful to trust the plan God had for her son, but I imagine her faith was tested in what lay ahead.

As mothers, we are no strangers to the battle between faith and fear. Faith and fear fight over the same space within us. They cannot overlap, but one can overpower the other. We are too easily consumed by fear, but fear is not of God.

> *God does not give us a spirit of fear and timidity, but of power, love and self-discipline.*
> 2 Timothy 1:7

Imagine the power, love, and self-discipline it took during the three months Jochebed kept her baby close to her, nursing him, cradling him, whispering to him, praying over him. We do this every day as our kids grow closer to being released into the world. Motherhood is not new. Our prayers for our children are not new. The things that incite fear in us are not new. The things that overwhelm us are not new.

Imagine the power, love, and self-discipline it took as her delicate touch lined the inside of the woven basket with tar. Taking her time. Covering it again to make sure there were no weak spots. Swaddling her baby boy. Knowing that in a few seconds he would leave her arms. Not knowing what was to come next. Not knowing God's plan. Not knowing an Egyptian princess would walk down and find her son, ignore her father's edict, and hire Jochebed to take care of her own son who would grow up as a Prince of Egypt. As a slave now earning pay, her life was changed. All the worry, the unknown, the fear, the anticipation, the hardships...and God said, "Do not fear. I've got this."

What does faith really look like when your last hope is to place your baby in a tar-lined basket in the Nile River (Exodus 2:3-4)? The NILE. The longest river in the entire world, home to crocodiles, venomous snakes, hippopotami, lions, and tigers, and bears, oh my. Okay, I'm not sure about the last three in Ancient Egypt, but you get my point.

I lived within a few miles of the Mississippi River for the first 21 years of my life, and I'm just going to put it out there that I do not think large rivers are very safe for babies. In my opinion.

It's a good thing my opinions do not matter much compared to God's.

As I began to dig deeper into the story of Jochebed, I realized I had a cartoonish vision of this moment in my head. As if it was no big deal, she put her baby in the Nile River. But now that I think about it, I don't fully trust inflatable floaties, much less a tar-lined woven basket. This story has a bigger impact on me now that I fully grasp the danger of the situation.

In Exodus 2:5-6, the Pharaoh's daughter discovered the baby crying. (Of course, NOW he cries. God thinks of everything.) Would the princess' heart break for the baby that was no ordinary child? By faith, Jochebed obediently executed God's plan, and Moses was returned safely to his mother's arms—a reunion only God could write into the story.

As mothers, we are all too familiar with Nile River moments. The times when we have to put our complete trust in God for our children's lives and for provision for our families.

When my daughter was eight months old, she contracted RSV, a respiratory virus that affects the lungs and causes breathing issues. For healthy older kids and adults, the symptoms are similar to the common cold, but it can be a serious illness for babies under a year old. Lena seemed to be getting better, and we put her to sleep in her crib for the night. Not long after, we heard her coughing, followed by horrible wheezing. The sound coming from her tiny body was what the doctors warned us would need immediate medical attention.

As soon as we put her in her car seat to head to the hospital, the unimaginable happened: she stopped breathing. My heart cried out to God. Though I was terrified, an unnatural calmness overcame me. I had no other choice but to fully rely on the Holy Spirit to put my body into motion. Otherwise, I would have been frozen with fear.

Within a minute (though it felt like eternity), the ambulance was on its way and she started breathing. It was labored, but she was breathing. My Nile River moment continued when she and I rode in the ambulance, both of us strapped to a gurney as I held an oversized oxygen mask over her tiny nose and mouth, but the worst of it was over. I felt God's peace overcome me as I hummed in my baby's ear to keep her calm. Her hoarse cries were a precious song of life and breath.

Each school year as I hand my babies off to a new teacher, I see myself at the bank of the Nile yet again. Jochebed's moment kneeling in the reeds is not unlike our own when we have to fully trust in God's protection over our families.

Without faith, fear would overcome our hearts.

What does this kind of insurmountable faith, trust, hope, and unfathomable love look like? Hebrews chapter eleven, the passage titled "Faith in Action," defines it as this:

Now faith is confidence in what we hope for and assurance about what we do not see.
Hebrews 11:1

Faith is an action step. It is blind belief and trust in our unfailing, all-powerful, all-knowing, and loving God.

Faith is releasing the instinct to take things into our own hands. Fortunately, we can find story upon story of faith throughout the Bible and in the testimonies of believers.

Although God is in the miracle-making business, there are some miracles we won't get to witness in our lifetime.

These were all commended for their faith, yet none of them received what had been promised. God had planned something better for us so that only together with us they be made perfect.
Hebrews 11:39

Many of the Israelites did not step foot into the Promised Land.

They did not live during the time when God Himself walked on earth as Jesus. And they did not see His ascent into heaven just as we have not yet witnessed the return of our King.

Sometimes we do not see the answer to our prayers, but perhaps our children will. Or our children's children.

We do not want you to become lazy, but to imitate those who through faith and patience inherit what has been promised. Hebrews 6:12

Each of these people in Hebrews 11, and throughout the Bible, played a part in God's story. In a theater performance, each of the people on the stage has her own role. If any one of them breaks character, she is not aligning herself with the purpose of the show.

The actor trusts that when the director tells her where and how to stand, what to do and when to do it, it will add to the overall composition of the scene.

We are characters in Jesus' story. God gives us each a purpose, and we're tasked to live it out as the Great Director designed.

Take a moment to get on your knees and pray to fully release to God anything weighing on your heart. Embrace His peace, assurance, and hope. Pray for the ability to imitate the acts of people in the Bible such as Jochebed who demonstrated faith in a seemingly impossible and inescapable situation. You are a child of God, and He has wrapped you in His wings (Psalm 91:4) to give you comfort and safekeeping. He safely delivers us in woven baskets and keeps us hidden from the enemy. Thousands of years later, His love still rings true and His story is not yet complete. He is using you for His purpose and has a plan continuing to unfold for generations to come. Trust Him. Let your faith overpower fear. Amen? Amen.

By faith Moses' parents hid him for three months after he was born, because they saw he was no ordinary child, and they were not afraid of the king's edict.
Hebrews 11:23

FAITH AT HOME

MASTER SCULPTORS

Use playdough or clay to mold different objects. Talk about how God's hands created them just as they are creating different things out of clay. With some types of dough/clay/putty, you can get a good imprint of your fingerprints.

> Yet you, LORD, are our Father. We are the clay, you are the potter; we are all the work of your hand.
> Isaiah 64:8

CHAPTER 4

TRAIN UP A CHILD

My husband and I decided our kids would attend public school. Obviously, as Christian parents, we are well aware the element of faith would not be present in their schooling. Topics such as prayer, spiritual warfare, serving others, obedience, self-control, and kindness guide conversations on our two-mile drive to school. I consider the moments before school crucial for their spiritual development. The last words they hear before the minivan door slides shut are simple reminders to help them shift their focus to God.

That and, "Wait! You forgot your lunch!"

When our oldest was in kindergarten, his teacher called to share a special moment from her class. The kids heard sirens pass by the school as an ambulance rushed to the hospital. James, never one to raise his hand, blurted out that they needed to pray for the person who was hurt. His sweet teacher initiated a moment of silence and allowed the students time to pray if they wanted. We often wonder if our kids will think about Jesus when they're at school—even more so in a school that does not teach about Him. We hope that what we teach sticks. That moment was an answer to our prayers. We continue to pray for those moments now that they are in middle and high school.

Moses had quite an eventful first few years of his life. He went from living with his enslaved Israelite family to living in a palace as a prince of Egypt. From being with people who loved him, to a strange new lifestyle with people who looked and sounded different from him. As a child, he was immersed into a community of people who did not believe in his God.

Egyptians did not share the same faith as the Israelites. Not even close. The ancient Egyptians practiced polytheism, the belief in many gods. They worshipped the Pharaoh because they believed he was delivered from the gods. Moses was taken from his home and his family to live in an Egyptian palace. He was educated in culture, language, and religion by idolaters and pagans.

I recently watched a video by Pastor Matt Chandler who suffered, and who is now healed, from brain cancer. After his diagnosis, Matt's fear wasn't that he was given two to three years to live. (In fact, he said his thoughts before his operation were, "I'm either going to wake up groggy in the ICU, or I'm gonna wake up in glory.") Instead, he feared his death would confuse his children.

He said, "The thing that would gnaw at me for the longest time was the thought that my kids would become embittered toward the Lord." He was afraid his young children might not hold on to their faith if God didn't heal their father.

I wonder if Jochebed had similar thoughts about being absent from Moses' life. She knew he would spend his most impressionable years separated from his fellow Israelites by palace walls, social class, religion, and freedom. His mother had trusted completely in God's plan to save Moses' earthly life, but what about his eternal life? How would Moses grow up to be a man of faith in the one true God, despite his Egyptian upbringing?

There are two things we need to remember. First, while we plant the seeds of faith, God makes it grow (1 Corinthians 3:6). God gently reminded Matt Chandler—and us—"I love your kids more than you do. Is your kids' salvation and their health dependent on you, or is it dependent on Me?"

That takes a little pressure off our shoulders.

Second, we are faith-ambassadors to our children. Before my freshman year of college, a team of upperclassmen called "ambassadors" took prospective students on a tour of the university. Their job was to tell us about the school and give a glimpse of campus life. We learned the history of the school and the ins and outs of college life. It was a deeper look into our new home.

Likewise, our role is to teach our kids about Jesus and share what a life with Him looks like. We have the opportunity to show them the path that can lead them to the threshold of an eternal life with Christ, but God opens the door and invites them into His kingdom. When we get wrapped up in the day-to-day, do we prioritize our roles as ambassadors?

Sharing His Story with Our Children

For Jochebed, the opportunity to raise her child in the ways of her people seemed lost until...

> *Shall I go and get one of the Hebrew women to nurse the baby for you?*
> Exodus 2:7

Pharaoh's daughter pulled the baby from the reeds. This is the daughter of the same man who gave the order to kill all Hebrew baby boys! As she held the baby in her arms, she had the choice to save him or align herself with her dad's proclamation. Moses' sister, Miriam, looked on and waited.

The princess must have seen what Jochebed saw when she gazed upon her son—this is no ordinary boy. The princess offered to pay Jochebed —a slave—to nurse the baby that the princess would adopt as her own.

Imagine Jochebed's reaction to that turn of events. Her short time with him would not just be for physical nourishment, but spiritual nourishment as well. Years later, Jochebed handed her son back to the princess to raise into adulthood.

It's easy for us to rely on the children's program Sunday mornings at church to teach our children about Jesus. However, faith training is part of our parental duty. The church's role is to reinforce and supplement what we teach at home. Or, we can use what we learn on Sunday morning to guide what we teach our kids throughout the week.

As we open our Bibles, our kids look on with interest. When we share what we know about God with our kids, they lean in close. We kneel before our Father to learn all of His ways and our children do the same to us, cuddling up to hear us share about God's goodness. The way our children trust us mirrors how believers put their trust in our Father. What a precious responsibility we have to be intentional about faith training.

Jochebed may have felt the pressure of a reduced timeline to spiritually train Moses, knowing one day she would hand him back to Pharaoh's daughter. I'm sure she wondered how she could build up her son's heart so it could withstand a culture that did not honor God.

Inevitably, our children will leave the comfort and protection of our nest by going to school, playing sports, attending a sleepover, or going to college far from home.

There will be a day when our kids face the outside world unaccompanied. Hopefully what we have taught them has a stronghold—in a good way—in their hearts.

> *Start children off on the way they should go, and even when they*
> *are old they will not turn from it.*
> Proverbs 22:6

> *Fathers, do not exasperate your children; instead, bring them up*
> *in the training and instruction of the Lord.*
> Ephesians 6:4

Jochebed did not have the Bible available like we do to serve as the handbook for faith while training Moses. When he was much older, Moses himself wrote the first five books of the Bible (Genesis, Exodus, Leviticus, Numbers, and Deuteronomy). Jochebed had only the knowledge passed down from her parents and the generations preceding her.

Moses' upbringing between two cultures benefited him in the long run. As an Egyptian prince, he received an advanced education that included lessons in languages and history. This education, along with the faith instilled in him throughout his young life, enabled him to grow into a strong leader.

Before he was even born, God chose Moses to redeem His people and free them from slavery. And God chose Jochebed to prepare Moses for that role.

Like Jochebed, the few short years we have to faith-train our children will fly by. If you have older children, you know this all too well. We are entering the driving years with ours.

Pray for us.

John Leyson once commented on the stretch marks strewn across my squishy tummy. He called them "tiger stripes." I excitedly told him how I got them. I love my stretch marks because they are a sweet memory of my babies growing inside me.

After Jochebed handed her baby over to Pharaoh's daughter, her stretch marks must have been a beautiful reminder of the time she spent carrying and caring for her son.

Our children leave marks on us. Even if you are not a biological mother, there is no doubt your children have left marks on you, maybe not physically, but emotionally.

Motherhood stretches our bodies, minds, hearts, and spirits as we teach and guide our children into adulthood.

Let my teaching fall like rain
and my words descend like dew,
like showers on new grass,
like abundant rain on tender plants.
Deuteronomy 32:2

As an adult influenced by this mother's early teaching and faith, Moses prayed these words when he led God's people on a journey to the Promised Land. Note the gentleness of his prayer. He prayed his words would wash over and rejuvenate the weary travelers. As a mom, I want the Word of God to be pleasant to my children's ears and rest peacefully on their tender hearts.

This is a beautiful prayer to remember, especially when we're tempted to use God's Word to rebuke, which we are called to do in "complete patience" according to 2 Timothy 4:2. For me, patience wears out quickly, so this is a reminder to be gentle in the way I teach my children. I catch myself disciplining because of my lack of patience, instead of disciplining for an act of disobedience. I discipline because I'm annoyed or inconvenienced, when the child hasn't done anything requiring a consequence other than a gentle reminder.

I have a lot of work to do.

When it comes to faith training, we can't teach what we don't know. But we gain more knowledge by teaching. Before I was a mom, I was a pre-kindergarten teacher. Do you remember learning to read? I don't, so I had to learn how to teach others to read. This led to understanding more about the English language which eventually led me to become an English tutor for English Language Learners who were stateside for college. I was in graduate school for a Masters in Education while simultaneously teaching in the classroom. Yet, I learned more through applying what I was learning in the classroom than when I was taught information.

As you teach your children about God, you will grow in your faith.

If we are intentional about instructing our kids, we will learn more because we are opening our Bible and finding new ways to explain things. Often, we know the perfect message for our children without realizing *we* need to hear it as much as they do. Maybe their angry outburst looks like our outbursts. Maybe their crossing boundaries at school is the result of witnessing us cross boundaries. Sometimes my kids sound exactly like me, and not in a good way.

We also can't keep what we are learning to ourselves. I love to steal away for some mama moments and keep my quiet time within the confines of my closet or my office. I also need to make a point to let my kids see me digging into God's Word. Not every time, but how else will they know it's important to me? How will I set the example for them if they don't observe me?

Although my husband and I often speak about God to our kids, use Scripture to emphasize a point in obedience training, and pray at mealtimes, we decided we still needed to be more intentional about faith training our children.

Faith training is less about direct instruction and more about showing and guiding our children through lessons in the Bible. Being intentional in training our children does not mean we simply read a story from the Bible or teach Bible facts via flashcards. Instead, we help our kids make connections through stories, games, songs, and activities. We like to call these Family Faith Activities.

In a Mary Poppins world, the children would sit obediently by my husband and me, completely devoted to the activity. Perhaps we would ask thought-provoking questions, or the kids would answer our questions with profound revelation.

In actuality, these nights are a bit of a train wreck (Get it? Faith *train*ing?), but somehow, my kids still seem to grasp what we are attempting to teach. And we do have fun. One thing is certain, these nights are nothing short of memorable.

In full disclosure, we are free spirits and do not stick to a schedule, though sometimes we try. We might plan for a Family Faith Activity every Tuesday in the month of May, instead of planning for every Tuesday forever. We know we won't stick to the rigidity long-term, but we can do anything for a month.

Take a look at your calendar. Choose a day and time that work well for your family. Pick a start date and an end date and stick to the plan. Find an age-appropriate curriculum or devotional online or at the local Christian bookstore to help guide you.

Or, simply reflect on Sunday's message at church and start a conversation. Don't know what to say? Then, start with a prayer asking God to lead the way. Trust Him to guide these moments.

Just because you've made a plan does not mean it will always go as you hope. Most often, our best faith discussions happen out of the blue in carpool, at the dinner table, or yes, even while I'm attempting to have some privacy in the bathroom.

Our goal to raise up the next generation of disciples is for Jesus Christ's name to be spoken and His Word taught within the walls of our homes.

God's love and salvation are what make His story the greatest one ever written! We are given the task to read and live out this story with our children so they can grow to do the same for generations to come. How amazing it will be to see your kids training your grandkids, who will in turn train your great-grandkids to be warriors for our Lord and Savior, Jesus Christ.

Spend time praying and planning about being more intentional in your faith training. If you're a new mom, pray God will guide you when it is age-appropriate. As your children mature, ask Him for opportunities to speak wisdom into their lives. And if an empty nester, consider mentoring a neighbor or young mom at church.

Fix these words of mine in your hearts and minds; tie them as symbols on your hands and bind them on your foreheads. Teach them to your children, talking about them when you sit at home and when you walk along the road, when you lie down and when you get up. Write them on the door frames of your houses and on your gates, so that your days and the days of your children may be many in the land the Lord swore to give your ancestors, as many as the days that the heavens are above the earth.
Deuteronomy 11:18-21

FAITH AT HOME

JOURNALING

Open a fresh notebook or staple blank pages together for you and the kids to design your own covers. Put on some worship music, turn to page one, and let the words flow. Journaling can also look like doodling, comics, bullet points, poetry, or more. There are no rules here.

Need a prompt? Pray for three! Pray three things for the world, three things for your community, and pray for three people you know. Or have your kids send a text message from your phone to someone you know to ask how they can be praying for them. Have them write a prayer for that person in their journals.

seek him first

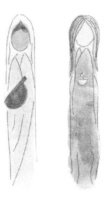

Blessed are those who keep his statutes
and seek him with all their heart—
Psalm 119:2

CHAPTER 5

THE RESPONSE

When the boys were little, I picked up two hobbies. I needed something besides folding onesies and cleaning up dried puree to spark a little joy during nap time. I started a blog called A *Tale of Two Kiddies*—a play-off of Charles Dickens' infamous A *Tale of Two Cities*. The blog's tagline was the same as the first line of the book: "It was the best of times, it was the worst of times." That's what you get when you're in the throes of sleepless nights and potty training.

When I wasn't writing, I was painting. I had so much fun painting murals in my son's nursery that I began painting nursery decor for friends and family. Pretty soon, I accidentally started a side business. People were referring me to paint murals and decor for their nurseries.

I kept busy by painting during nap times and mealtimes when they were strapped in their highchairs. During bath times I'd paint next to the tub. Sometimes I'd bounce a baby on my left knee while painting with my right hand. I always regretted it the next day when I'd stay up way past my bedtime to finish one more commissioned piece.

Somewhere during that time, God called me to ministry to lead a Bible study group for moms. Instead of dropping everything to follow His calling, I added it to my busy plate. That, and teaching art at the local university. And more volunteer opportunities. And by then, I had added our caboose to our family.

I became part hat stand, part clown, as I started juggling all the different hats I was wearing.

And not well, mind you.

When burnout was on the horizon, I had the opportunity to expand my business to delve into product design, baby bedding, home decor outside the nursery, children's clothing, and more.

By this time my heart wasn't in it, but I pushed forward.

Then right before our huge launch, God told me to shut down the business. And just like that, it was over. I heard Him loud and clear, and I didn't fight it this time.

I felt a huge weight lifted as I surrendered my newfound time to Him.

For a few years, God had persistently nudged me to write. I had written a bit here and there, but not with the urgency I was hearing from Him.

I was so busy volunteering at church and school, teaching art at the local university, chauffeuring kids around, and running a home business—all good things—that I didn't have time for what God wanted me to do.

The good things seemed harder and more stressful than they should have been. They felt like a constant uphill battle. And then I had an epiphany: "Just because I think it's good, doesn't mean it's God."

God and I needed a heart-to-heart on how to free up time so I could make myself available to accomplish what my Father was calling me to do. I had peace knowing He would call other people to serve in the areas from which I was stepping back.

We cut back on extracurricular activities as a family, and I stopped teaching art. (*For now*, God said). As for the home business? *I have bigger plans*, He said. He needed me to focus on growing His ministry and He needed me available *now*.

Our lives are a back-and-forth between our responses and God's responses. I learned the hard way that it's our responsibility to seek His will, listen, and respond back to Him.

The stories of two women in the Bible—Hagar from Genesis and the Shunammite woman from 2 Kings 4—took place over a thousand years apart. While their journeys share similarities, each woman responded differently to adversity.

The next four chapters compare their journeys, how (or if) they sought God during difficult times, and God's response to each.

Hagar and Sarai

In Genesis 15:5, God promised Abram he would have children as numerous as the stars in the sky. From generation to generation, Abram's descendants would fill the earth. In the next chapter, his wife, Sarai, questioned the likelihood of bearing children since she was well past her child-bearing years. Like, *well* past. At 90, Sarai made a plan to side-step God's plan.

God had chosen Abram and Sarai to grow His kingdom. Sarai couldn't see beyond her limitations and the seeming impossibility of it all, so she took matters into her own hands instead of waiting for God.

> *So she said to Abram, "The Lord has kept me from having children. Go, sleep with my slave; perhaps I can build a family through her." Abram agreed to what Sarai said.*
> Genesis 16:2

Not only was Hagar living in slavery, but then Sarai forced her into a situation that would leave Hagar's life in turmoil. Hagar resented Sarai; Sarai resented Hagar. Feelings of jealousy, contempt, anger, and regret reared their ugly heads.

When I read the stories of these women in the Bible, I try to understand the scope of their animosity toward one another. A friendship would not likely be birthed between slave and slave owner. While you and I can't directly relate to a relationship formed under those circumstances, we have experienced those feelings of jealousy, contempt, anger, and regret within our own relationships. I have both felt them and been on the receiving end with friends.

The situation and the strained relationship between Sarai and Hagar left Hagar convinced there was no way out, so she fled. She and I apparently have similar conflict resolution skills, because I would have done the same.

Most of us respond to adversity in one of three ways: confront the problem, ignore the problem, or flee from the problem. But with each of those responses, we attempt to deal with the problems ourselves instead of taking them to God.

When I wrestled with anger toward one of my friends, I ignored the tension for too long, turning my anger into bitterness instead of forgiveness. When I was on the receiving end of gossip and bullying, I ran from the problem, never addressing it with the "friend" who caused it.

As someone who identifies as a peacekeeper, confronting an issue is difficult for me, though sometimes I rise to the challenge. In each of these scenarios, I jumped into a response before kneeling before God in prayer. *God, how should I respond? What should I do?*

Hagar chose response number three.

Sometimes we run from a situation because we think we would rather be alone than work through the problem. We want to close the door and never look back. By doing so, we sometimes choose a path that God has not intended for us.

When Hagar fled, she did just that. She did not reach out to God before fleeing. Fortunately, God travels alongside us. He is there to guide us back to the path He laid for us.

> *The angel of the Lord found Hagar near a spring in the desert;*
> *it was the spring that is beside the road to Thur. And he said,*
> *"Hagar, slave of Sarai, where have you come from, and where are*
> *you going?"*
> Genesis 16:7-8

God found Hagar and met her exactly where she was. He knew where she came from and where she was going but wanted her to respond.

Perhaps this is a question He wants us to reflect on often. Are we on His path? Where did we come from and where are we going?

As Christians, we are on a journey from sinfulness to righteousness, but often we shift our focus toward shiny things and squirrels. We juggle too many hats and wear busyness like a badge of honor instead of honoring God in our work. Do the answers to these questions align with what God has planned for us? Are we falling deeper into sin and farther from God? Where were we before we met God, and are we heading back to that place?

Hagar opened her eyes, opened her heart, and listened to God as He told her to go back. God knew it would be a hard road to travel. It wasn't a perfect haven—it wasn't even pleasant—but her obedience would lead to a promise.

> *The angel of the Lord also said to her: "You are now pregnant and you will give birth to a son. You shall name him Ishmael, for the Lord has heard of your misery."*
> Genesis 16:11

The name "Ishmael" means "God hears." God heard the affliction, misery, weakness, despair, bitterness, anger, and suffering Hagar felt. Oftentimes, when we feel we can't go any farther, God listens. He promises to shoulder our suffering and carry us through.

> *Cast all your anxiety on him because he cares for you.*
> 1 Peter 5:7

Hagar named the spot where God spoke to her *Beer Lahai Roi*, meaning "the well of the Living One who sees me." Still today, God meets us right where we are. He speaks to our hearts. And, like Hagar, He sees us through the loving lens of a Father who also happens to be the One who created us. He sees us like no one else does—the best version of ourselves, who He knows we would be if we walked in His ways. He offers us the opportunity to go back to where He wants us. *Where are you going? Go toward Me. Seek Me.*

Walking toward Him doesn't ensure a smooth and level path. He doesn't promise a life without pain and suffering. In Genesis 16:12, God told Hagar that her child would be a "wild donkey of a man" and "will live in hostility." To me, that sounds like toddlerhood and the teenage years in a nutshell. God warned Hagar that her son wouldn't simply grow out of the stage of animosity. He told her things would not be easy, but she had to go back.

Hagar obeyed and returned to her life with Abram and Sarai (Genesis 16:15-16). She may have attempted to take a detour, but ultimately her obedience put her back on His path. I—and maybe you, too—can relate.

Why would God tell Hagar to go back into slavery? If we solely look at the first part of this story, we have a hard time understanding how God could allow her to live under these conditions.

But in Genesis 17:11-26, we discover that Ishmael receives the covenant of circumcision at the age of thirteen alongside his father. Abram's name changed to Abraham that same day. If Hagar hadn't returned, Ishmael would have been cut off from this covenant. Her return allowed this holy agreement to physically mark him as a descendant of Abraham. God did not let her suffering go to waste.

Hagar and Ishmael left soon after with God and Abraham's blessing. In Genesis chapter 25, Ishmael returned home for his father's funeral. He and his brother, Isaac, buried their father together. Because Hagar had obeyed God, Ishmael also had a relationship with his father, joining him in the covenant with God for the blessing of a great nation.

Ishmael then grew up and twelve tribes were formed from his sons, just as there were twelve tribes of Israel from Isaac's grandsons through Jacob. The Ishmaelites, descendants of Ishmael, became tribes of Gentiles. The New Testament recounts a covenant which applies not only to the people of Israel, but also to us, the Gentiles, who believe in the redeeming blood of Jesus Christ.

But whoever drinks the water I give him will never thirst. Indeed, the water I give him will become in him a spring of water welling up to eternal life.

John 4:14

FAITH AT HOME

STARING CONTEST

Two people. One person smiles while the other one tries to not crack a smile. When he or she finally smiles, talk about how faith is contagious just like smiles and laughter.

> A *cheerful heart is good medicine, but a crushed spirit dries up the bones.*
>
> Proverbs 17:22

CHAPTER 6

THE GIFT

My kids think they live in a republic, a democracy. They state their demands, and by unanimous vote, pass their decrees. Only, they never factor in my veto power. Each summer they lobby for no chores, no summer reading lists, no errands, and absolutely "no fun-less or boring activities."

So naturally, when I mentioned our need to go grocery shopping, I braced myself for the protests to ensue. My rehearsed retort was at the ready.

Instead, my oldest came in with a goofy grin on his face, clutching a mason jar filled with the kids' collective birthday money. I immediately knew what that meant—a twist of intentions I should have seen coming: a request to visit the toy aisle.

Ugh.

My archnemesis with all its overpriced, cheap plastic. There was already enough of it scattered all over the floor of my home.

Two large, expectant brown eyes stared at me. Though he wasn't saying a word, I could hear his plea: *Please say yes. Please say yes. Please say yes.* My urge to veto hung in the balance.

Desperate not to have to deal with complaining or feet dragging in the store, I said yes. My hopes for a quick shopping trip were dashed. Instead, it would be filled with indecisiveness, or more likely manipulation, as my oldest son would use his powers of persuasion to coerce his younger sibling into buying what he really wanted. It's an all too familiar scene. The manipulation would lead to a chorus of whines when the younger two realized they were not getting what they wanted.

In anticipation of the meltdowns that were sure to come, I was already annoyed before we walked out of the house. I clutched the wheel and was in full-blown lecture mode during the drive to the store and our trip through the aisles as I first gathered the things on my list.

The kids excitedly kept up and over-praised my grocery choices. I suspected they were overplaying the pleasantries so I wouldn't change my mind.

I lapped up and down the toy aisle barking snippy reminders and "hurry ups" to my kids, pointing to the milk in our basket in need of refrigeration. The kids were well-behaved and kind, and thrilled at the chance to spend their own money.

Shortly before they decided what to buy, I realized I was missing a golden opportunity to watch my kids simply be kids. They were having fun, giggling and bright-eyed, soaking in every minute of the shopping experience. And I was missing out. At some point, in the hustle and bustle of everyday life, I failed to remember the preciousness of my three hand-knit blessings before me.

I struggle to be joyful in those moments. I often prioritize productivity over recreation thanks to the never-ending to-do list.

Do you remember the day you found out you were going to be a mom? What did you feel? Disbelief, excitement, nervousness, joy—each emotion fighting for the spotlight as glimpses of the future flashed before your eyes. Your life forever changed the moment you glanced at the positive pregnancy test, answered the phone call from the adoption agency, or received approval to become foster parents.

Now, imagine God personally delivering news that you would become a mom. Both Hagar and the Shunammite woman received the promise of a son from an angel of the Lord and a holy man of God respectively. God spoke to and guided these women in their motherhood journeys, despite where they were in life. He does the same for us today.

Hagar's Gift

The angel of the Lord found Hagar and shared God's promise

with her. The gift of a child blessed Hagar, despite the daytime drama showdown between her and Sarai. God's presence and His promises comfort us amidst hurts and brokenness.

Even when we want to run from the pain of our circumstances, God follows us to bring us back to Him.

> *So Hagar bore Abram a son, and Abram gave the name Ishmael to the son she had born.*
> Genesis 16:15

If this story was about your family, what would verse 15 look like? Reread it, but instead of reading it with Hagar, Abram, and Ishmael's names, insert the names of you and your family. You and your family *are* written into God's story like those on the pages of Scripture.

The Shunammite Woman's Gift

The Shunammite woman's story is about her encounter with a prophet named Elisha. Prophets were messengers of God who performed miracles through the power of the Holy Spirit. Before his predecessor, Elijah the prophet, died, Elisha asked to receive a double portion of Elijah's spirit (2 Kings 2:1-15). First came EliJAH, then came EliSHA. Confusing, right?

In 2 Kings 4:8-9, the Shunammite woman describes Elisha as "a holy man of God." Her description of him is unique because this is the only time a prophet is called *holy* in the Old Testament.

Elisha's holiness came from God's Spirit which was passed from Elijah to him. The Shunammite woman recognized Elisha's holiness and prepared a special place in her home to house him when he came to town.

On one of his visits, he called on her to repay her for all she had done for him (v. 13). The Shunammite woman lived quite a different life from Hagar. She was a free woman, with a husband and a home, wealth and comfort. She lived a life of contentment.

If a prophet of God asked what could be done for us, how many of us would reply, "Thanks, but I'm good"? I'd probably say something along the lines of, "Do you have a pen? It will take me a minute to write it all down."

My day is full of prayer requests to God for health for my family and friends, for financial stability, for the safety of my kids and husband, for my house to clean itself...

I even pray for contentment. I think I'd like to take a cue from our friend here and say, "You know, God. Today? Today, I'm good."

We can all learn a thing or two from this unnamed woman. She is described as "wealthy" and at first glance, desired nothing beyond what she already had. But even women with all the money in the world have secret desires tucked deep into their hearts. And though she didn't mention it to Elisha, something was missing from her life.

A *child*.

Specifically, *a son* to carry on the family's legacy and inheritance. Elisha, filled with the Holy Spirit, was able to bless her with the promise of this incredible gift.

Though she knew him to be anointed by God to perform miracles, she feared deception and an empty promise (v. 16). Her response suggests she had come to terms with the fact that she may never become a mother.

Infertility is a heartbreaking struggle for many women. You may have experienced the deep sorrow of a negative pregnancy test, or many. Perhaps you are in the depths of it right now.

With so many well-meaning family and friends in your life, their attempts to share comforting words may begin to feel like false hope.

The Shunammite woman had given up on becoming a mother and feared disappointment. It can be easier to take hope off the table—accepting it will never happen. And sometimes that's God's plan, but other times, He's waiting for the perfect time to surprise us with a miracle.

The Shunammite woman already had a testimony of God's faithfulness before Elisha showed up at her door. She was content and had nothing to ask of him. But now, her story continued beyond what she believed it would.

She gave birth to a son a year later, exactly as Elisha had promised.

Our Gift

Children are a heritage from the LORD, offspring a reward from him.
Psalm 127:3

Heritage is an allotted and valued portion passed down from one generation to another. Children are one of God's greatest tangible gifts. They are an inheritance created by His own hands. Your children may or may not be a product of your own womb, or may not live in your own home.

Each child in your life carries on a bit of your legacy whether you are an aunt, grandmother, teacher, stepmother, or honorary mother. God has entrusted them to us to raise our children (they *will* arise), not only to have good manners, say kind words, and lift the toilet seat (although this ranks high on my list of things to teach my boys), but also to grow up to know and serve our precious and loving God.

Often I overlook the gift part and only see the "gray hair" moments. You know, the ones when you literally feel another hair slowly fading to gray from root to tip, such as the one-hundredth reminder to listen the *first* time, the "he's looking at me" arguments, and the grape jelly all over the new rug.

I do not always have the gentle and patient reaction of a godly woman in these moments.

My gold-star parenting days are those when my mind, heart, and spirit are all set on the glory of God. When I depend on Him for guidance, strength, and patience, I am fulfilling the role of motherhood according to His calling.

Those are the days when the words pouring from my mouth are strewn with God's words, when they speak of grace, and glory, and joy, and peace, and holiness. It's a choice I make to keep Christ at the center of my choices.

On those days, I see the magnitude of the grace and love that came in the form of my little, God-wrapped gifts. Through me they have the opportunity to learn about an incredible inheritance into a kingdom of glory.

This intangible, eternal gift also came in the form of a tiny and delicate baby—Jesus.

Just as God had promised a son each to Hagar and the Shunammite woman, He also promised a son to Mary. And *that* Son had been promised to all of us long ago to bring freedom, redemption, and salvation to God's people. Though you may know these verses by memory, allow them to drip into your heart word by word.

> *For God so loved the world that he gave his one and only Son, that whoever believes in him shall not perish but have eternal life.*
> John 3:16

For it is by grace you have been saved, through faith—and this is
not from yourselves, it is the gift of God.
Ephesians 2:8

Because God loves us, he offers salvation to us through His Son. His grace covers us, and He asks only for our faith in return. As we make room in our hearts for Jesus to dwell and surrender ourselves to Him, He will grant us the greatest of blessings: eternal life free of pain, tears, sin, and suffering. God sees us and knows us. And despite our flaws and failures, He loves us deeply. Salvation is the greatest gift.

When you pray today, approach God with thanksgiving. Ask God to help you understand the fullness of His gift of salvation. Wouldn't it be amazing to wake up each morning with that reminder on your heart? Live each day internalizing the enormity of the gift. It will transform your life, my friend.

FAITH AT HOME

GIFT EXCHANGE

Put each family member's name on a piece of paper, fold it, and place it in a jar. Each person picks a name from the jar and creates a handmade gift to give to that person. Give the kids access to random materials such as straws, empty toilet paper rolls, buttons, and the usual craft supplies to create a one-of-a-kind treasure. Wrap and exchange the gifts. Discuss what kinds of gifts God gives us.

Every good and perfect gift is from above, coming down from the Father of the heavenly lights, who does not change like shifting shadows.

James 1:17

CHAPTER 7

THE JOURNEY

My spiritual journey is closely related to my motherhood journey, and I don't think I'm alone. When my oldest son was six months old, I joined my first Bible study group. I had been a Christian for seven years, but my Bible still had a fresh-off-the-shelf look to it. No crinkles in the spine, no scribbles in the margins. I regarded it like one of my Spanish textbooks from college—or maybe Biology. A foreign language.

Too embarrassed to be seen looking through my table of contents to find the different books in the Bible, I almost didn't show up to the group Bible study. Though I had put my faith in Christ as a teenager, I hadn't even taken the first steps to truly follow Him. My faith aligned with a do-good checklist, not the heart of Christ.

When I began to learn how to read the Bible and how to apply

God's Word to daily living, my eyes were opened to the majesty of God. I also now had a Christ-centered community with over fifty women to help guide me.

Before I accepted God's gift of salvation through Jesus, I was blind; after I made that decision to turn from sin and follow Him, I could see.

As soon as my journey with Him began, I grew more like Him in my thoughts, words, and actions (theologians call that ongoing process "sanctification"). Finally, I saw God's magnificence in full color. Seeking God by delving deeper into His Word exponentially improved my God vision.

The more I learned about God, the more I felt "in tune" with Him. His presence became familiar to me. Before reaching out to people to complain, freak out, and gain sympathy, I sought out my Father who sees me. The Holy Bible replaced the how-to parenting books that had previously been stacked on my nightstand.

Scripture tells me He sustains me, holds me in His hands, and covers me with His wings. That truth wrapped its way around my tender heart as I began to put my trust in my Father. Spiritual growth happened during midnight feedings, rocking babies, and tummy time—and both the joyful and messy motherhood moments in between.

For Hagar and the Shunammite woman, motherhood took them on a spiritual journey as well.

Hagar's Journey

Hagar gave birth to her son, Ishmael, just as the angel of the Lord had promised. Unfortunately for Hagar, life would not get easier for her or her son.

He will be a wild donkey of a man; his hand will be against everyone and everyone's hand against him, and he will live in hostility toward all his brothers.
Genesis 16:12

I know many families who have faced challenges in parenthood: health diagnoses, learning disabilities, developmental delays, behavioral disorders, and physical disabilities among their children. It often feels like the world is against them as they juggle insurance, health care, medications, school systems, therapies, and more. The uphill battle is steep and bumpy for these families. And yet, the trials do not outweigh the love they have for their children.

Hagar still welcomed the blessing of a child, knowing what those challenges would be for her and for him.

Abraham was 86 years old when Ishmael was born and 100 years old when Isaac was born. The half-brothers were fourteen years apart.

During Isaac and Ishmael's time, it was customary for the eldest son to inherit all his father's possessions when the father died. As the elder brother, Ishmael threatened Isaac's inheritance. This weighed heavily on Sarah's heart, but God always has a plan that is bigger than we can imagine in our present circumstances. Though God had always intended to build a nation through Abraham and Sarah's son, He did not forget Hagar and Ishmael.

> *I will make the son of the slave into a nation also, because he is*
> *your offspring.*
> Genesis 21:13

This verse shares God's promise and helped Abraham put his sixteen (plus) years of trials in context to focus on God's bigger picture. As outsiders who are reading Hagar's story from start to finish in a matter of minutes, we see God's plan unfold.

For Hagar, living in the moment, I imagine the plan was not so clear. When she left, she had no direction but to get far away. She was given only food and water to carry on her shoulders with her teenage son by her side. Finally, she was free. But where could she go?

There was a sense of hopelessness to Hagar's wandering with no end in sight. She came to rest at the point of exhaustion and desperation in the Desert of Beersheba.

> *When the water in the skin was gone, she put the boy under one*
> *of the bushes. Then she went off and sat down about a bowshot*

away, for she thought, 'I cannot watch the boy die.' And as she sat
there, she began to sob.
Genesis 21:15-16

Resigned and defeated. Faced with a mother's greatest fear. All
hope was lost, and she had nowhere to go. Stripped of all basic
needs for survival, she was helpless as she tried to cope with her
circumstances. Her aimless wandering ended as her tank ran dry.
The sound of her sobs fell flat on the sand as the desert terrain
extended beyond her line of sight.

Under either similar or different circumstances, have you ever
reached the place where despair presses in? Have you felt
desolation hover over you like a cloud, concealing hope? It's hard to
see God in these moments and it's easy for us to give up pursuing
Him (or as Psalm 63:8 calls it "following hard after Him" or "clinging
to Him"). But when we let despair win and when we give up the
pursuit, we cannot move forward in our faith. Spiritual growth
comes to a halt.

At this point in Hagar's journey, she succumbed to despair.
There was nothing left for her to give to sustain herself or her son;
only God could rescue and restore them.

The Shunammite Woman's Journey

Like Hagar in the desert, the Shunammite woman faced a

heartbreaking moment with her son. As she held her lifeless son in her arms, her response to tragedy was a far cry from Hagar's. Instead of being immobilized by grief, she held on to hope and took action.

> *She went up and laid him on the bed of the man of God, then shut the door and went out.*
> 2 Kings 4:20

I imagine her distraught but determined look as she closed the door behind her. There was no time to entertain questions. She didn't even tell her husband that their son was dead. The Shunammite woman sought out the holy man of God to come to save her son, bypassing the puzzled looks from her husband and Elisha's servant.

> *"Everything is all right,"* she said.
> 2 Kings 4:26

Everything was not alright by our standards, but was *all right* by God's. Her statement wasn't just assurance to calm her heart or theirs. It was truth. A firm declaration of faith. *Everything is all right.*

The Shunammite woman's son was dead, but she knew that there was only One who could breathe life into death. When she arrived at Elisha's location, she fell to her knees and "*took hold of his feet*" (verse 27). The Shunammite woman chose to *weep forward*, meaning that even through her sadness, she sprang into action. She was single-minded in her pursuit of God who—through Elisha—would bring healing to her son. Step by step, her faith drew her closer to God and He stayed by her side. That growth and that journey is sanctification.

Our Journey

> *For this very reason, make every effort to add to your faith goodness; and to goodness, knowledge; and to knowledge, self-control; and to self-control, perseverance; and to perseverance, godliness; and to godliness, mutual affection; and to mutual affection, love. For if you possess these qualities in increasing measure, they will keep you from being ineffective and unproductive in your knowledge of our Lord Jesus Christ.*
> 2 Peter 1:5-8

Spiritual growth is a slow transformation, not an instant overhaul.

> *Do not conform to the pattern of this world, but be transformed by the renewing of your mind.*
> Romans 12:2

Just as the Shunammite woman "went up" and "went out" (2 Kings 4:20), we will "add to" (2 Peter 1:5) and "be transformed" (Romans 12:2) in "increasing measure" (2 Peter 1:8) as we walk with God. These building blocks in 2 Peter 1 are the milestones we reach on our journey as His Word begins to bear fruit in our hearts. As we study the Word of our Father, we gain wisdom and understanding. Trusting God and seeking Him first become second nature, instead of an afterthought.

This transformation isn't hard work, it's holy work. It's how we blossom into our role as Christ-centered mothers seeking to help our children rise up to follow Him. It happens within the walls of our hearts and homes as we live in Christ and walk humbly with the Lord.

Whoever claims to live in him must live as Jesus did.
1 John 2:6

We will never be perfect in our walk with Christ, but take heart. God will meet us where we are on our journey and walk with us the rest of the way. How can our journey with God help us survive parenting?

Having a closer relationship with God helps us through sickness, tantrums, diapers, discipline, whining, and the dreadful days of potty training. He picks us up and carries us through trips to the hospital, devastating diagnoses, the challenges of having a child with disabilities, losing loved ones, infertility, miscarriages, overwhelming stacks of bills, troubles at school, job loss, big life decisions, mental overload, and the list goes on.

Our relationship with God is our best, and sometimes only, resource. On the days when I want to give up and hide in my closet eating the world's chocolate supply, I am strengthened by Him. God eases my stress and anxiety and helps me put my mommy brain and God lens back into focus. He shows me the big picture about the role He has selected me to play, and it helps me be a better parent.

Ask God to continue to bless your journey as you seek to know Him more. While we will all stumble through our Christian walk and motherhood, thank God for His faithfulness to meet you where you are and for giving you the greatest role in the world.

FAITH AT HOME

FAMILY VERSE

Choose a family life verse. Our family's verse is Philippians 4:8-9. If you need help choosing one, search "Bible verses for families" online or search through different themes in a Bible app.

Activity ideas:

- Using strips of paper, write the verse and wrap them around everyone's wrists like bracelets.
- Use chalk to write the verse on your driveway or sidewalk.
- Hang a paper or sticky note with the verse by the head of everyone's beds.
- Use a dry-erase marker to write the verse on your bathroom mirrors.
- Write a Bible verse on painter's tape and stick it to the doorframe of your home. (Variation: use sticky notes or tape a verse to your door).

Fix these words of mine in your hearts and minds; tie them as symbols on your hands and bind them on your foreheads. Teach them to your children, talking about them when you sit at home and when you walk along the road, when you lie down and when you get up. Write them on the doorframes of your houses and on your gates...

Deuteronomy 11:18-20

CHAPTER 8

THE WELL

Depleted. Defeated. Drained. Those are the words that come to mind after a hard day of *momming*. Fifteen years ago, a hard day meant rocking a tired infant who staged protests against his drooping eyelids. Ten years ago, it consisted of juggling tantrums and potty training with one, breastfeeding and spit-up with another, and a daredevil who liked to climb all the things. And now, a hard day is breaking up sibling fights, sassy attitudes, running nonstop from one place to another, disciplining, disciplining, disciplining, and balancing the scale of sheltering my children and teaching them about the real world. All hard stages, different challenges, same well run dry.

I imagine our sisters in the Bible faced many of the same child-rearing challenges, but without the luxuries we have today such as sound machines, breast pumps, and air conditioning. It wasn't until well after I became a mom that I took notice of these mothers of the Bible, mulled over their family genealogies, and grasped how their faith was threaded from generation to generation. For Hagar and the Shunammite woman, each faced defining moments where God met them in a remarkable way.

Hagar Receives the Well

As Hagar wandered through the desert with Ishmael, her food and water were depleted. I try to imagine the scene: the desiccated air, parched throats, hunger pangs, shielding their eyes from the sun to see nothing but the vast expanse of desert before them, exhaustion winning over, their bodies protesting against taking another step...

Hagar left her son under the sparse shade of a scrawny bush and walked away. She didn't abandon him, but sat far enough away that they could likely not hear each other cry (Genesis 21:15-16). As far as she could see, they were alone in a wasteland. A wave of hopelessness overpowered Hagar. A mother mourning the imminent death of her son. There was nothing for her to do, nowhere for her to go, no way for her to save her son, *Ishmael*—"God hears."

God heard the boy crying...
Genesis 21:17

I wonder if Hagar thought she would meet God again on her journey? Had she questioned the promises from the Lord from all those years earlier? This baby was to grow into manhood, God said, yet, he lay there dying before her eyes.

In many circumstances, we can't fathom how things can change. Our brains are wired to believe what we know from experience. Hagar was aware she and Ishmael could not survive without food and water. Their bodies could not physically carry them farther. Common sense told her there was nothing more that could be done. But faith is believing that God can do beyond what makes sense to us. Where was her faith?

Though our faith may waiver, God never leaves our side. He heard Ishmael's cries; He called out to Hagar.

...and the angel of God called to Hagar from heaven and said to her, "What is the matter, Hagar? Do not be afraid; God has heard the boy crying as he lies there."
Genesis 21:17

I love God's reassurance to Hagar as He called her by name. God speaks to His children tenderly and knowingly. "*What is the matter, My daughter? Do not be afraid.*" He assures us that He is beside us and presses a gentle reminder in our hearts—we are His daughters.

God hears our cries and knows everything about us. He calls us His children. God doesn't stumble through our names, running through a list of His kids until He lands on the correct one like I do when my kids are in trouble. He doesn't fumble His way through how best to speak to our hearts, as I often do when comforting my kids. He gets it right every time. With Him by our side, what is there to fear?

In Genesis 21:18, God instructs Hagar to *"Lift the boy up and take him by the hand."* Imagine the steps Hagar took to walk back toward her son. Or did she run? As my newly-turned teenager stood next to me earlier, the thought occurred to me: Ishmael was likely close to her size if not bigger than Hagar at this point. She lifted him up and held his hand in hers. This verse is a beautiful picture of motherhood—a mother's hand grasping her son's, leading him step by step toward hope.

God has sent us on this mission of motherhood. He tells us daily to lift up our children, comfort them, and take them by the hand to guide them. He does the same for us.

Our role in our children's lives mirrors God's role in our own lives. He lifts us and holds our hands. Our Father opens His arms, initiating a precious relationship with each of His children—you and me included.

Then God opened her eyes and she saw a well of water.
Genesis 21:19

When Hagar was broken, in despair, and felt she had nothing

left to give, God hand-delivered a life-giving answer to her. He placed a well full of water at her feet.

Hope. In that moment, Hagar was able to refill her skin *and* give her son a drink. A well of water brought life and nourishment to Hagar and Ishmael—first filling her wineskin, then his.

First your oxygen mask, then the kids'.

We can only pour into our children when our own cups are full. When we are filled with the Holy Spirit, we are best able to comfort, guide, and discipline with God-minded love. The closer I am to God, the better I parent. My family can see a difference in me.

But I have a confession to make. Some days the enemy wants to take over, and I let him. I wallow, I stress, and I let frustration control my relationships with my husband and children.

Other days, I wake up with my eyes focused on God, praising Him, and His peace floods my weary heart. On those days, my eyes are open to see the well placed before me. I take a drink. I fill my cup. I then reach down to fill their cups because I have more than enough to give, thanks to God.

Those are the days I shower my children with love, snuggles, grace, and gentle instruction.

There's a reason why the flight attendants tell passengers to place their oxygen masks on before placing one on a child. Our minds are clearer then, and we are better able to help our children when we can take a breath.

First, we must see the well before we can draw water from it.

Take a moment to pray this prayer: *God, open my eyes to see the well before me. Fill my cup so I may drink. Let it overflow so I may give my children a drink. This is my prayer to You.*

The Shunammite Woman Goes to the Well

The Shunammite woman had a different reaction to tribulation than Hagar. Hagar dropped to her knees with hopelessness, while the Shunammite woman set into action.

As mentioned earlier, she wept forward in her pursuit of God. Her husband and Elisha's servant wondered, "What is the matter?" but she knew this was out of their hands. She had nothing to fear as she set on her path to the one who could help.

When she arrived to meet Elisha, she fell at his feet. From her knees, she cried out to him. Although Elisha was filled with the Holy Spirit, he did not rush to the woman's son. He sent his servant ahead and Elisha stayed by the woman's side the entire time.

God never abandons His children. The Shunammite woman's despair spurred her into swift action to seek Him and Him alone. When we are feeling most broken and on the edge of falling apart, we can take refuge in God if we seek Him.

The Shunammite woman walked back home toward her son, and Elisha followed. He was behind her, positioned to catch her if she fell. She never looked back to see if he was still there—she simply trusted.

Her belief in Elisha's presence sets an example for our faith walk with God. We do not need to see Him to know that He is there every step of the way.

"Surely God is my salvation;
I will trust and not be afraid.
The Lord, the Lord, is my strength and my song;
he has become my salvation."
With joy you will draw water
from the wells of salvation.
Isaiah 12:2–3

Dear God, may I always run toward You. May You walk ahead of me, beside me, and behind me to guide me, comfort me, and catch me when I fall. May Your living water flow freely from You, bestowing life and nourishment to me and my family. This is my prayer to You. In Jesus' name.

Sometimes, God brings the well to us as He did with Hagar. Other times, God wants us to take action, to run to the well like the Shunammite woman.

Take heart, sister. There is a well to refresh and revive you so you can continue your journey. Sustenance comes from the living water that flows from God Himself.

To him who is thirsty I will give to drink without the cost from the spring of the water of life.

Revelation 21:6

Then the angels showed me the river of the water of life, as clear as crystal, flowing from the throne of God and of the Lamb.

Revelation 22:1

Take a moment to praise God. Seek first God's kingdom. Ask Him to fill your cup from His living well which flows from Him and His Son. Make this a daily practice. As His river flows deep into your heart, witness His abundant blessings. I pray that your well is overflowing today. Pour out its refreshing waters upon your husband and children and watch them drink in His living waters, too.

F A I T H   A T   H O M E

S E L F   P O R T R A I T S

Everyone draws a picture of themself. Take turns as each person describes themself. Have your child choose a color and write the attributes he/she sees around his/her portrait. The kids will likely come up with physical traits. Then it's your turn, Mom. Using another color, write the things that you know about your child that he or she may not even know about themself (kind, smart, brave, etc.). This shows them all the many ways God knows them and how He loves them.

Variations:

- Mirror Talk: Use dry-erase markers on the bathroom mirror

- Draw body outlines with chalk on the driveway

- Use a dry-erase board or chalkboard

- Paint on a canvas

Get creative!

May our Lord Jesus Christ himself and God our Father, who loved us and by his grace gave us eternal encouragement and good hope, encourage your hearts and strengthen you in every good deed and word.

2 Thessalonians 2:16-17

follow him

Blessed are all who fear the Lord,
who walk in obedience to him.
Psalm 128:1

CHAPTER 9

GENERATIONAL OBEDIENCE

Have you ever looked at your kids and thought: "Where on earth did they learn that?" "Who did they get that from?" Have you wondered what type of behaviors your kids are picking up from you? When our kids do or say things that are completely, well, weird or inappropriate or disobedient, Bo and I joke: "That's *your* kid."

Here's a prime example: my oldest, James, is a button pusher. No button is safe. One time I was checking out at Home Depot when the alarm system started wailing throughout the store. I looked down to see James-the-toddler standing behind the cashier with his finger hovering over the theft-alert button, a look of innocence on his face. The sirens echoed on and on, and the poor cashier didn't have a clue how to turn it off.

Another time I was so excited to exercise my right as a U.S. citizen to vote in the presidential election. Inside the poll booth, the electronic ballot lit up before us with the flashing green "vote" button in the corner. As I explained to toddler James about the process and privilege, I heard the all-familiar *bee-dee-da-boop* of a cast ballot. My ballot. Before I got a chance to select a candidate.

That's my husband's kid. Likely, he'd say that's *my* kid.

Our kids pick up quirks and behaviors from each of their parents. Fear of bugs, for example. Here in South Louisiana, we have stinging caterpillars. They are as terrifying as they sound. I stepped on one as a child, which only confirmed and intensified my fear. I have instilled this fear in my children, especially John Leyson, who fears wasps. It might be because of the look I get on my face when I spot one nearby. His fear was confirmed when he got stung and now he relates that to every flying bug he encounters and to shots at the doctor's office.

His fear triggered an epic meltdown when we took Lena to get her ears pierced because she was getting "shots in her ears." He didn't want his sister stung. Fortunately, she was determined not to show a hint of weakness to prove that she is the brave one.

Our kids also pick up our likes and dislikes. My kids love skies and chasing sunsets like their mama, and they love robotics and Star Wars like their dad. Our team loyalties have been passed down to our kids because they see the euphoria we get when our team wins—and the disappointment when they lose. They love to root for LSU football because it's Mom's team and Oklahoma because it's Dad's team. In 2020 we made shirts that cheered on both teams in the national championship game because the kids were so torn over who to cheer for—Mom's team or Dad's? By the way, my team won. I'm not gloating or anything. Just stating facts here, folks.

Team loyalties. Is part of the legacy we're building a sense of loyalty to God's team, to His people, His Church?

What impact does our faith have on our children? As I studied the women listed in the Matthew chapter one genealogy, God continuously highlighted the rippling effects of "generational obedience." I saw a common thread of faith and obedience to God that connects each of these mom stories together, from generation to generation, pointing directly to Jesus.

Through the stories of Tamar, Rahab, and Ruth we find a history of obedience, trust, and love—fundamentals of faith passed down from parent to child. The historical differences of time and culture, while dissimilar to our own, teach us a great deal about God and His kingdom. Inheritances and legacies held higher stakes in Old Testament times than they do today. Personal possessions were passed down to the Israelite's children, and their children, and their children's children.

We do still pass items or treasures through generations. My grandmother gifted me with the diamond from her engagement ring before she passed away. I have some of my great-grandmother's artwork, furniture made by my grandpa or passed down from my great-grandmother, and my grandfather's backpack from World War II (all these years later, it still smells like it has been through a war).

The crib my grandmother Lena bought for me has also been used for my sister, several cousins, and my kids. My beloved dollhouse was a Christmas gift from my grandmother Pat. My dad restored it after it was nearly destroyed in Hurricane Katrina. What a privilege it was to pass it on to my daughter on her sixth birthday.

Each of my kids is named after family members. The family line holds James Arthur I, II (my husband), and now the III (my oldest). John Leyson I, II, III (my dad), and now my middle son. Lena Marie is named after my grandmother.

Legacy means a lot to me. But really, it is our legacy of *faith* that is of eternal value and matters most to God. In the Old Testament, the two were tied together.

Summers at White Bear Lake Mamie would sit in the living room, very early in the morning, a shawl around her and Bible on her knee. Who of my grandchildren will carry this on?
- Great-Grandma Gay

Years after I became a Christian, I had an "aha" moment about the Bible: "This book is a history book!" Why it took me years to figure that out, I have no idea. Perhaps because I'd spent the majority of my time reading Paul's letters to all of the –ians (Corinth*ians*, Galat*ians*, Ephes*ians*...) and not enough time reading Numbers (because who has?).

More specifically, after I became a mother, the genealogical threads throughout the Bible changed my spiritual journey in a groundbreaking way. The names no longer became lists I could safely skim through. Instead, my eyes rested on each individual name. Fathers and sons—and there were more names, the names of mothers and grandmothers, written between the lines. My name, and my children's names, and my grandchildren's names, and those of their children would be added to this long list one by one. We are all a part of a story that began long ago.

The revelation and my new role as a mother also made me realize I was no longer concerned with my obedience to God just for my own sake. My obedience to God, and likewise my disobedience, can and will have generational consequences.

The spiritual significance of motherhood awakened in me as I pored over these lines of genealogy. Timelines, maps, and family lineage piqued my interest as I began to piece the biblical puzzle together.

I now had a deep-seated desire to learn more about what God specifically placed in the Bible to reach the hearts of His creations. I became a "Book" nerd in the best possible way.

Generational Obedience

What is generational obedience? Put simply, it is a pattern of obedience to God that is passed down from generation to generation. It is the God-honoring obedience we teach our children.

Our children then go on to practice and teach their children. As Christian parents, our role is to pour faith into our children. Our prayer is they decide for themselves to follow Christ as well.

> *I have no greater joy than to hear that my children are walking in the truth.*
> 3 John 1:4

I am the daughter of a prodigal daughter. My mom didn't find her way back to Christ until years after I first met Him. Because of my mom's disconnect with Jesus, I remember a time in my life when I did not know who Jesus was. I had heard about Him, but He seemed more like a storybook character instead of, you know, *God*.

We moms have an incredible opportunity to make sure our kids never have to remember a time when they did not know about Jesus. Perhaps they will remember that we, their mothers, were the first ones to tell them about Him.

What does your faith lineage look like? Who taught you about God? Was your faith passed down from one generation to the next, or are you a first-generation Christian?

The New Testament opens with the genealogy of Jesus. I like to read Matthew 1:1-16 out loud, even though I'm likely mispronouncing names. I may have attempted to rap this chapter a few times, but that'll be our little secret. Saying the Bible characters' names helps me see the greater picture of Jesus' family tree.

Matthew's genealogy is the only one to mention women...*mothers.*
Just like you and me, they each had a story and played a role in the
lives of their children and descendants. Though Matthew lists the
genealogy from the bloodlines of the fathers, as was the custom of
the day, he takes extra care to mention five special mothers. I love
this sweet celebration of motherhood.

Judah the father of Perez and Zerah, whose mother was Tamar...
Matthew 1:3

Salmon the father of Boaz, whose mother was Rahab, Boaz the
father of Obed, whose mother was Ruth...
Matthew 1:5

David was the father of Solomon, whose mother had been Uriah's
wife...
Matthew 1:6

And Jacob the father of Joseph, the husband of Mary, and Mary
was the mother of Jesus who is called the Messiah.
Matthew 1:16

Matthew was a tax collector before he became a follower and
disciple of Jesus Christ. A numbers and details guy. He knew he
needed to prove to unbelieving Jews that Jesus was indeed the

prophesied Messiah. He chose his first words to be a family tree that points directly to Jesus, the Anointed One.

And, so no one would be mistaken about their role, he included the women whose obedience to God paved the way for the Messiah. Their faith journeys are chronicled in the Bible. Their stories are not pretty. The lineage of Jesus is not one of jewels and riches like one would expect of a King. His family line is not full of prominence, refined bloodlines, famed aristocracy, and pureness that would make anyone boast about his or her ancestors.

Three of these women weren't even Jews. They were Gentiles adopted into the kingdom through their obedience to God. The stories of the women in Matthew chapter one were tainted, just as ours were before we met Christ.

All the same, we know they were mothers and their paths were part of God's plan. Their obedience—their faithfulness to God's teaching and guidance—was life-transforming not just for themselves, but for the generations of children that came after them.

Our children are watching our every move. They see and hear us even when we think they aren't looking or listening. We are the ones who model adulthood for them. Our children carry a part of us in them throughout their entire lives: the good, the godly, the bad, and the ugly. Truth time: which of those do you think your children most see on the daily?

But the fruit of the Spirit is love, joy, peace, forbearance, kindness, goodness, faithfulness, gentleness and self-control.
Galatians 5:22-23

Who wouldn't desire these godly characteristics? They make the greatest impression on our family. Do we always get it right? Not even close. But the closer we follow Jesus and the more we get to know our Father, the easier it is for the fruit of the Spirit to flow through us and out of us.

In Matthew's genealogy, we don't see perfect people, but we do see how their obedience to God ignited a legacy of obedience for generations: generational obedience. For some of us, it started with our ancestors, our grandparents, and our parents. For others, it starts with our generation.

My maternal grandmother used to listen to the Bible on her tape recorder. Even in her final days, when she stopped eating and slept most of the day and night, the audio version of the Bible was running on the cassette player. I didn't understand it then, but now I do. I want to hold on His Word to until my last breath and I want my kids to have that same desire. "Her children arise."

Heavenly Father, may our faith in You be passed on from generation to generation. Through our obedience and trust in you, may our kids see You in and through us. As we live in You, may they learn to love as You love. God, prepare our hearts as we continue to learn more about You. In Jesus' name we pray, Amen.

FAITH AT HOME

FAMILY TREE

Draw a family tree that goes back as far as you can rattle off in your head. It can be a simple chart on a piece of paper, or pull out the paint, construction paper, glue, and markers to make it a piece of art. Tell your kids stories from when you were a child or stories that have been passed down from generation to generation.

> *If you belong to Christ, then you are Abraham's seed, and heirs according to the promise.*
> Galatians 3:29

CHAPTER 10

THE FAMILY SEAL

Sitting on the sidelines for one of our boys' soccer games, I told my youngest her feet could not cross the line onto the field. So she did what any pig-tailed, three-year-old boundary-pusher would do. She stood on the line, her toes touching the edge, but not crossing it. To emphasize that she was doing exactly as she was told, Lena bent her torso and waved her hands over the line while keeping her feet firmly planted.

She wanted to be a part of the game but wasn't yet allowed to participate. She had to wait until she was old enough to receive her own team jersey. Or get crafty and wait for the ball to cross into her territory outside the playing field as she so desperately hoped.

Now that she plays team sports, she comes to each game with the same expectancy. Lena's basketball team was full of all-stars.

She wasn't one of them. She could have easily blended in with the bench. Instead, she spent the games hopping up and down in front of the coach saying, "Put me in, Coach!" Her team won the championship that year and she has the medal and jersey to prove it.

Though she wasn't the star of the team, her hard work and enthusiasm made her a valuable teammate.

Tamar

(Note: At least two Tamars are named in the Bible. Their stories are different. This Tamar's story is found in Genesis 38. The other Tamar's story is even more heartbreaking.)

Tamar is often seen as a boundary-pusher. *Canaanite. Seductress. Deceitful.* These labels have dragged Tamar through the mud for millennia. She was discarded as unworthy and evil in the eyes of her father-in-law, but her patience, intellect, and expectant attitude changed the game.

Judah recognized them and said, "She is more righteous than I..."
Genesis 38:26

Our western lens has emblazoned a scarlet letter on the heart of a woman who ultimately kept Judah from falling deeper into sin and restored his family line that would in time birth the Savior of the world.

God imprints another image on the hearts of His children.

Living in the twenty-first century A.D., we are culturally removed from the lifestyle and regime of those who lived in the Eastern world during the nineteenth century B.C. The events in Tamar's story do not make sense in today's culture, so we have a hard time seeing her as righteous. Tamar was a rule follower, even if it seems to us like her feet stood right on the line of the playing field.

Beginning in Genesis 37, Judah was the older brother of Joseph who suggested to his brothers that instead of killing Joseph for the "crime" of being their father's favored son, they should sell him into slavery. Because, after all, "He is our brother, our own flesh and blood." (Genesis 37:27). How "kind" of Judah.

In Genesis 38, Judah then left his brothers and grieving father to stay with his friend Hirah, where he met his Canaanite wife. He got married and had three sons: Er, Onan, and Shelah. In early Old Testament times, fathers would often select spouses for their children. Generally, this matchmaking would benefit the entire family. The bride's and groom's families would enter into a covenant of marriage in which they would pass on an inheritance. With the proper betrothal, this would ensure the acquisition of additional wealth and property for both families and their future generations.

Notably, Judah's father had not been a part of his own wedding arrangement. This is our second indication that Judah was falling out of step with God. (The first being when he sold his brother into slavery.)

Judah played matchmaker between his oldest son, Er, and a Canaanite woman named Tamar. Because Er was wicked in God's eyes, he died, leaving Tamar without a child. She then married Er's brother, Onan. The marriage between a widow and her late husband's brother was called a Levirate marriage. In Latin, *levir* means brother-in-law. The brother-in-law essentially inherited his deceased brother's wife and kept the wealth within the family.

> *If brothers are living together and one of them dies without a son, his widow must not marry outside the family. Her husband's brother shall take her and marry her and fulfill the duty of a brother-in-law to her. The first son she bears shall carry on the name of the dead brother so that his name will not be blotted out from Israel.*
>
> Deuteronomy 25:5-6

After the death of Judah's son Er, followed by the death of his son Onan (yes, he was evil, too), the covenant of Levirate marriage was to be carried out through Judah's youngest son, Shelah. At the time, he was too young to be married. Judah, now a widower himself, had no intention of carrying through with the covenant that was God's law for His people even when Shelah was of age. He blamed Tamar for the deaths of his sons. Judah sent Tamar back to her father, though Tamar's dad had no legal obligation to take his daughter back under his roof after the exchange of marital vows and dowry with Judah's oldest son. Tamar was cast to the sidelines.

The implications for both Judah and Tamar were incriminating if Judah did not fulfill his family's side of the covenant. To publicly declare that Shelah would not honor the Levirate law would have brought disgrace on his name. Without an official end to the covenant, Tamar would not be allowed to remarry outside of Judah's line and would remain a childless widow. But if she had a child outside of Judah's lineage, that child would have been able to potentially claim Judah's inheritance since Tamar was Judah's daughter-in-law. This would be dangerous for Tamar and the child.

Israel was a country defined by race and religious beliefs in addition to geographic boundaries. Therefore, God created these all-encompassing commands to protect the genealogical lines of the Israelites and make the nation thrive. God's people knew His law. Knowing God's law was their way of knowing Him. And Judah's line was at risk of being blotted out of Israel...until Tamar stepped in (Deuteronomy 25:6).

After the death of Judah's wife, Tamar became the matriarch of Judah's family. When she heard where Judah was going, she knew his intentions. Prostitution was rampant in Canaan and sheep shearing was lucrative for the men. The prostitutes waited by the road as the men came to do business. Tamar took off her widow's clothes and, veiled, waited for Judah. The veil was strictly for concealment and was not typical attire for prostitutes. Though Judah didn't recognize Tamar, she kept him from falling deeper into sin because she was still bound to his family as a wife. She kept his seal, cord, and staff to prove her identity.

These were no everyday trinkets. Judah's seal was used as his identification. Likely the seal was cylindrical or disc-shaped, with Judah's family insignia or signature on the flat end. In the ancient world, it was worn around the neck with a cord threaded through a small hole.

> *Speak to the Israelites and get twelve staffs from them, one from the leader of each of their ancestral tribes. Write the name of each man on his staff.*
> Numbers 17:2

Judah's staff signified him as the leader of his household. Later it would be passed down from heir to heir to set apart the leaders of the tribe of Judah. What Tamar held—to prove her identity as the mother of Judah's children—would be the same seal, cord, and staff that would one day be theirs.

She wasn't interested in monetary gain, but to once again have a place among God's people. To establish a legacy within His kingdom. To live a life of promise, instead of a life of promiscuity.

Tamar knew the implications should he suspect that she was pregnant by any other man. Judah's seal would be the mark of her righteousness.

With the children she bore, his staff could now be passed down to a new generation.

The scepter will not depart from Judah,
nor the ruler's staff from between his feet,
until he to whom it belongs shall come
and the obedience of the nations shall be his.
Genesis 49:10

Though the laws of the Old Testament were created to lay the foundation of a nation before Jesus' coming, God has always opened His home to those who come to Him.

Even to a veiled Canaanite who was considered unworthy, He deemed her righteous. He found Tamar worthy of being written in His book for eternity.

Through His Son, Jesus Christ, both Jews and Gentiles are welcomed into His family under His seal.

And it is God who establishes us with you in Christ, and has
anointed us, and who has also put his seal on us and given us his
Spirit in our hearts as a guarantee.
2 Corinthians 1:21-22

Jesus marked us with His seal to identify us as His. His Spirit sets us apart as we follow the Good Shepherd and His staff. We are blessed by His righteousness and His legacy is what we hope to pass down from generation to generation.

I have been reminded of your sincere faith, which first lived in your grandmother Lois and in your mother Eunice and, I am persuaded, now lives in you also.
2 Timothy 1:5

According to Paul, God's plan for Timothy began with seeds planted by the sincere faith of his mother and grandmother. Tamar's faith birthed another generation to carry out God's legacy.

When the time came for her to give birth, there were twin boys in her womb. As she was giving birth, one of them put out his hand; so the midwife took a scarlet thread and tied it on his wrist and said, "This one came out first." But when he drew back his hand, his brother came out, and she said, "So this is how you have broken out!" And he was named Perez. Then his brother, who had the scarlet thread on his wrist, came out. And he was named Zerah.
Genesis 38:27-30

Tamar may have been unjustly sidelined, but God's plan was always for her to be a major player in the game. Though Tamar was a foreigner, marrying into Judah's family meant that she and her children became indoctrinated into the lineage of God's chosen people. She fought hard for the seal that would eventually belong to her descendants, Joseph, and Mary, the mother of Christ.

Heavenly Father, may your seal be passed on for many more generations as we lay the foundation of a Christ-centered home. May our children always desire to be on your team, eager to follow your lead. Please bless our home and the hearts that grow within it. Amen.

FAITH AT HOME

MUSEUM TOUR

Take a museum tour of your home. Point out different heirlooms in your home that were passed down from one generation to the next. If you don't have any family heirlooms, perhaps you have a piece of furniture you picked up from a garage sale. Make up a fun, pretend history about that item. For added fun, if it's at night, turn off all the lights and use a flashlight on your tour. Or if it's during the day, use an object like a hairbrush to represent a microphone.

> *In his great mercy he has given us new birth into a living hope through the resurrection of Jesus Christ from the dead, and into an inheritance that can never perish, spoil, or fade. This inheritance is kept in heaven for you...*
> 1 Peter 1:3-4

CHAPTER 11

BY FAITH

Mom Prep 101. My syllabus said to get all the parenting books. *What to Expect When You're Expecting* topped the pile on my nightstand, followed by *What to Expect the First Year*. This book series saved a lot of calls to my OB because as a first-timer, I had all the questions. "This baby is freaking out right now! What is he doing? Oh, oh... that's just hiccups...or maybe gas."

When I was a new mom, mom blogs became "the thing" and with them, polarized opinions on parenting styles. These blogs changed the face of motherhood. A new type of judgment set in: mom-shaming. Mom-shaming is a faceless beast hiding behind perfectly staged façades. Moms were suddenly only a blog post away from being awarded the distinction of *#badmom*.

After scrolling the internet from one blog to the next, it hit me: I was turning first to Google instead of God for parenting advice. I did not trust my God-given parenting abilities to raise the children that God Himself had knitted together in my womb. I put more faith in the abilities and opinions of other moms who wrote a post that went viral—because surely a million shares signal it's good parenting advice. Even my husband couldn't convince me I was doing a good job because the book, the blog, or the meme said I was doing something wrong.

No blog post on parenting has ever radically changed how I parent. If it's good, it gets a thumb's up—*click*—and if it's really good, a share on social media. Even if my blog had millions of followers, dozens of awards, and critical acclaim, it shouldn't be someone's resource, textbook, instruction manual, or how-to guide for life. The Bible is that text. It may not have the how-to on potty training, but it is God-breathed. The Bible is alive and relevant even today. Its words have life-changing power.

When I first opened the Bible as a new Christian, I read it as if it was a blog post. I would read a few verses and think, "Wow, that's good stuff." I'd also skim through the boring or confusing parts and then not use it in the way it is intended for me to learn and grow. It wasn't until I jumped into my first Bible study that I learned to give the Bible the attention it deserves.

In that study, I was taught the importance of breaking verses down to better understand them, checking out cross-references, and memorizing Scripture. I began to pray Scripture out loud, meditate on what God was speaking to me through His Word, and seek understanding in areas that were unclear. With these skills, the Bible became the tool I needed to transform me and a sword to arm me for spiritual battle. At that point, I realized the real-time relevance of this Book that would serve as my companion for the rest of my life on earth.

Though I've yet to find a passage that talks specifically about diaper rashes, ear infections, co-sleeping, first crushes, or failure to turn in school assignments, it does indirectly offer advice for rashes, infections, tenderness toward children, guarding our heart, and faithfulness to assignments. And the Bible is packed with stories of faith-driven victories. When we read about these heroes of faith, they teach us to turn to our Father instead of social media. With God as our guide, we become the mothers He intends us to be, which often looks different from the latest parenting fads and trends.

Rahab

By faith the prostitute Rahab, because she welcomed the spies, was not killed with those who were disobedient.
Hebrews 11:31

Moses led God's people out of slavery in Egypt and through the desert for forty years. He died before they entered the Promised Land. His successor, Joshua, was the one to take the final steps to lead the Israelites there. Joshua's first task was to conquer Jericho, so he deployed spies to scout out the city in preparation for creating a military strategy. In Jericho chapter two, the spies entered Rahab's home. Apparently, they weren't very sneaky spies because the king of Jericho immediately found out. Rahab hid the spies and lied to her king.

> *I know that the LORD has given you this land and that a great fear of you has fallen on us, so that all who live in this country are melting in fear because of you.*
> Joshua 2:9

In Exodus 23, God made a promise to Moses to rain "terror" (v. 27) on His enemies. News of the Israelites' miraculous victories at the hand of God had reached the ears of all of God's enemies. The people of Jericho were "melting in fear" because they knew they were defenseless against God's mighty power.

Rahab professed her faith to these men she had just met. She knew where her salvation lay—in the God of her enemies. She committed treason against her king by putting her life and her family's in God's hands. She trusted God's protection more than the protection of her king. Turning her back on her people, their sins, and their false gods, she put her life in the hands of the God who led His people to conquer their rightful land.

I know my profession of faith and putting my trust in God did not resemble the Lifetime drama affair that Rahab's did. My story would read like this: "So she sat down on a metal folding chair across from two friends and prayed to God..." No spies, no espionage, no sign of the king's men with swords knocking at my door. Yet, the stakes were just as high for me as for Rahab: eternal life or death.

Rahab's testimony of bravery and God's faithfulness is the only explanation for her survival. Presumably, at the time Jericho fell, Rahab was not a mother. With one mention of her name in Jesus' genealogy, her story culminated with a marriage to an Israelite man, and the birth of a child. She and her family had a new life among God's people.

Salmon the father of Boaz, whose mother was Rahab.
Matthew 1:5

Can you imagine what Rahab's faith trainings with Boaz and her other children looked like? *One day, these two men came knocking on my door and I knew right away that they were men of God. So I hid them away to not be found by the king and his men... and that is how I became one of God's people.*

She was a hero among the Hebrews because her daring trust and unwavering faith in God's protection prevented Joshua's spies from being caught. As Christians, we often use faith and trust interchangeably, but there are subtle differences. Faith is knowing

God as Creator, Father, Protector, Defender, etc. We don't need evidence for faith, just unquestioning belief. Faith allows us to have a relationship with God.

On the other hand, *trust* is when we have evidence and knowledge to believe God's abilities will provide for, protect, strengthen, and sustain us because of His deep love for us. Trust requires action. It requires us to "let go and let God."

Trust is a hard thing for our kids to visibly see in us because we rarely openly discuss big adult things with them. They just see the outcome of our decision-making. They don't see us wrestle with anxieties and fears and then release those to God. We do a pretty good job of hiding that part of our lives.

We teach our kids how to trust God by giving credit to God everywhere we see Him move. And, bonus—that'll help to open our eyes to his blessings as well. As we share our fears and how we turn those over to God in prayer, our kids see a strong, confident, and brave woman before them—a mama who trusts that her God will protect her and her family.

If we have faith without trust, it means we haven't completely surrendered ourselves to God. Trust without faith means we don't believe in God, but put our trust in other things. Rahab's faith and trust in God trickled over from generation to generation.

We see this in the character of her son Boaz before he married Ruth (Ruth 2:12) as well as in her great-great-grandson, David, before he defeated Goliath with a single stone (1 Samuel 17:37). Her faith and trust were then carried out through her great-great-great-grandson Solomon as he sought wisdom from God (1 Kings 3:7-9). It overflowed into the rest of her genealogical line all the way down to Joseph, who married Mary and became the adoptive father of Jesus Christ (Matthew 1:24-25). Generations begat generations of faith and trust.

The fall of Jericho is chronicled in Joshua 5:13-6:27. Rahab and her family waited as instructed within the walls of her home as the Israelites marched around their city for seven days. Then trumpets sounded in the distance accompanied by shouts from their former enemies. The walls crumbled around them with a deafening roar. Their lives were miraculously spared by the mark of a scarlet cord, and they lived the rest of their lives among God's people. The Israelites were still nomads at the time with more land to conquer.

As the first generation of Israelites entered and settled in the Promised Land, Rahab joined their ranks. Having lived and worked in an established city, Rahab and her family would have been instrumental in building the foundation of a newly settled society. At the same time, she still had a lot to learn about the rituals, celebrations, commandments, and laws of her former enemies.

Because of her faith and trust in God, and her obedience to follow the detailed instructions of the spies, Rahab's story is part of history—His story—and is heralded among other heroes of faith in Hebrews 11. Are there people in your life whom you consider heroes of faith? Perhaps your parents or grandparents, pastor, friend, or mentor? Do you consider these people heroes of faith because they believe in God or because of how they live out their belief? Do these people demonstrate their faith by trusting in God to equip them as they navigate life according to His will?

The book of James tells us about faith and deeds and begs the question, "*What good is it, my brothers, if a man claims to have faith but has no deeds?*" (James 2:14)

> *You see that his faith and his actions were working together, and his faith was made complete by what he did.*
> James 2:22

I find that my children often turn a deaf ear toward the words that come out of my mouth, but they certainly watch my every move—and remind me what I'm doing wrong, the little darlings. If I only repeat words from the Bible but do not actively put them into practice or show God's love and kindness to others, then my faith will confuse my children and those around me. When we trust God, we obediently act upon our faith and give Him the glory in the end.

> *In the same way, was not even Rahab the prostitute considered righteous for what she did when she gave lodging to the spies and sent them off in a different direction? As the body without the spirit is dead, so faith without deeds is dead.*
> James 2:25-26

I encourage you to read Hebrews 11 out loud, emphasizing "by faith" each time it is written. If quiet time today is surrounded by your little ones, let them crawl into your lap as you read Hebrews to them. Pray that your faith is like Rahab's when she put her trust in the true God. May they see their own mom written on the pages of Scripture as their hero of faith.

FAITH AT HOME

STAMP OF APPROVAL

Using a stamp pad, put each person's fingerprints on a white sheet of paper. Compare them and talk about their differences. Discuss how every one of God's children is unique but made in His likeness. See if you can each recreate your own fingerprints by drawing them on paper.

> *So God created mankind in his own image, in the image of God he created them; male and female he created them.*
> Genesis 1:27

> *For you created my inmost being; you knit me together in my mother's womb.*
> Psalm 139:13

CHAPTER 12

A COVENANT OF LOVE

Puzzles are great for a child's development of spacial awareness, shape recognition, and fine motor skills. A toddler's first puzzle is typically made of wood with spaces cut out to perfectly fit each piece. The pieces themselves have a wooden peg sticking out the top for little fingers to grip securely. It takes a bit of banging, twisting and turning, testing different pieces, and grunts of frustration before toddlers make the connection between the shape of the piece and the shape of the hole it fits in.

When my kids worked through their first puzzles, I'd hand them one piece at a time and encourage them to look at the shape, find its space, and keep turning, turning, turning...there! Their eyes would light up when the piece slipped into place.

Life is a jigsaw puzzle. Picture it with me. God has a completed puzzle of our lives and hands us one piece at a time. Sometimes, that piece is rounded and smooth and fits seamlessly into our lives. So seamlessly, that we don't realize it was placed there by the hands of our Creator. It just *is*.

Other times, God hands us a jagged piece that doesn't seem to fit no matter which way we turn it. We place this puzzle piece aside and say, "This was not part of God's plan." Or we try our best to reshape that piece and hammer it into a space where it doesn't fit.

Over time, as other pieces fill in and we can see more of the picture, we realize how perfectly that jagged piece joins each facet of our lives together. The piece creates a noticeable junction where change, progress, growth, and divine power are evident.

> *"For I know the plans I have for you," declares the LORD, "plans to prosper you and not to harm you, plans to give you hope and a future."*
> Jeremiah 29:11

Ruth

So much happened after Rahab's family acclimated to life under God's command. God faithfully delivered His people into Canaan—the Promised Land. But it didn't take the Israelites long before they strayed from God. A famine blanketed the land of milk and honey. Families like Naomi's went in search of provisions.

The account of Ruth the Moabite takes place one generation

after Rahab's. At first, Naomi saw Ruth as one of those jagged puzzle pieces. She wasn't quite sure how her daughter-in-law fit, so she tried to put that piece aside. Fortunately, God is the puzzle master. As the pieces began to fill in around her, a bigger picture was revealed—a foreshadowing of a Redeemer who was to come. Ruth's story is a reminder that our stories are each uniquely designed and intricately orchestrated by God.

Salmon the father of Boaz, whose mother was Rahab,
Boaz the father of Obed, whose mother was Ruth,
Obed the father of Jesse,
And Jesse the father of King David.
Matthew 1:5-6

Because of a famine, Elimelech and Naomi moved their family from Bethlehem in Judah to Moab, a country across the Dead Sea from Israel. Elimelech died, and each of her sons married Moabite women. Then her sons died as well. When the famine ended in Israel, Naomi decided to return to her people in Bethlehem. She encouraged her daughters-in-law to go back and live in Moab with their families, marry Moabite men and start a family with them, but Ruth refused. She followed Naomi back to Bethlehem.

But Ruth replied, "Don't urge me to leave you or to turn back from
you. Where you go I will go, and where you stay I will stay. Your

people will be my people and your God my God. Where you die I
will die, and there I will be buried. May the Lord deal with me, be
it ever so severely, if even death separates you and me."
Ruth 1:16-17

Naomi is broken, "bitter" (v. 20), and "empty" (v. 21), yet Ruth
stays by her side. Her first act of obedience. Ruth's love for Naomi
parallels God's love for us, even when we ourselves are broken,
bitter and empty. Ruth offered Naomi companionship when she had
none, taking care of her emotional needs in addition to her physical
ones.

When I think about Ruth, I picture my friends who are nurses.
They give everything they have for the needs of the sick. I envision
those around me who are caregivers for their elderly or disabled
loved ones. But mostly, I see mothers—women who have given up
sleep, independence, sanity (I'm right there with you), clean homes,
and sometimes careers of choice to care for their children.

Ruth gave up her home and everything she knew to follow
Naomi back to Bethlehem. Her sacrificial love led her into the arms
of God. It is with His strength and guidance that Ruth followed
Naomi. The details that unfold—piece by piece—can only come from
God's good and perfect plan.

"As it turned out" (Ruth 2:3), Ruth stumbled upon Boaz's fields to
pick grain left behind by the harvesters—another of God's divine
interventions—and Boaz offered her drink, food, protection, and

God's blessings. He had heard rumors about this foreigner who gave up everything to take care of Naomi.

> Boaz replied, "I've been told all about what you have done for your mother-in-law since the death of your husband—how you left your father and mother and your homeland and came to live with a people you did not know before."
> Ruth 2:11

Because of Ruth's kindness to Naomi, Boaz showed Ruth the same kindness. This is the perfect model of God's love for us and how He blesses us in return for our kindness. God knew all too well that Boaz, son of Rahab the Canaanite, would come to the aid of another foreigner. He got his protective instincts from his mother.

By her luck, if there was such a thing, Boaz was a relative of Naomi—a kinsman redeemer. (Another piece added to the puzzle.) A kinsman redeemer was the male relative who provided protection and well-being for the wife of the deceased. By taking her into his home as his wife, he took on the responsibility of the late husband's land and assets. Their firstborn would be able to receive the full inheritance of the late husband. In this case, Boaz and Ruth's son received Elimelech and Naomi's legacy. Does this sound familiar? This fell under the same Levirate marriage law that allowed Tamar to still have a stake in Judah's inheritance.

Full circle spoiler alert: We women no longer need to rely on the Old Testament kinsman redeemer to take care of us, because Jesus has fulfilled that role for us all! And now, the biggest inheritance we can pass down to our children is the love of Jesus Christ.

Through the offspring the Lord gives you by this young woman, may your family be like that of Perez, whom Tamar bore to Judah. Ruth 4:12

This family had already seen the faithfulness of the Lord to their family. And we have the pleasure of seeing a bird's-eye view of God's sovereignty. We could not have dreamed up this perfect ending.

The book of Ruth opens and closes with new beginnings and blessings from God. The picture took shape, revealing divine interaction by the hand of God. The Maker restored the fortunes of the land and ended the famine (Ruth 1:6). By the end of the book, Boaz and Ruth got married and the Lord blessed them with a son. God's covenant with Abraham continued through the birth of Obed. From famine to fortune, from broken to whole, and from death to life.

Know therefore that the LORD your God is God; he is the faithful God, keeping his covenant of love to a thousand generations of those who love him and keep his commandments. Deuteronomy 7:9

As He keeps His covenant of love, we follow His commandments to love. How to love God and love people is passed down from us to our children—as is how *not* to love.

Our kids hear us complaining, they hear our hatred and our bitterness. They know when our heart refuses to forgive. They hear our gossip and our distaste for certain people. Our children imitate how we both love and lack love. When we complain, show disrespect, belittle others, or gossip, we challenge our own integrity and we make it okay for our kids to do the same. We have the power to warp our children's minds into thinking that we are better than others around us simply by how we show or don't show love. Instead, let our love for others speak loud enough for our kids to hear.

Recently my son gave me a compliment that is a testament to those who came before me. He said, "Mom, you make friends wherever you go. We walk away and the cashier is your new friend. It's everywhere we go." I get that from my mama who got that from her mama. My grandmother Lena was known for being able to make friendly conversation wherever she went. I have inherited that through the example set before me and now I see my kids— especially her namesake—doing the same.

My husband and I serve as international mission team leaders at our church. When we travel to Haiti, our mission is to extend Christ's love to the people we meet. It's easy to do when you're on a mission high—when that's your purpose for the week. But what about when we get home? Do we remain steadfast in our mission?

Do we push our needs aside and seek out those who are struggling? Do we invite the homeless, the addicts, the poor, the disabled, the widows, the orphans, the elderly, or the godless into our hearts to be in community with them? Do we open our arms to give warm embraces to strangers on the streets?

Ruth's sacrificial love extended beyond a week abroad. As did the love of her kinsman redeemer, Boaz, who abandoned his own inheritances for Naomi's.

God shared this story with us so we, too, can imitate their examples of His mercy, humility, grace, and love.

Obedience, trust, and love are all fundamentals of our faith. But I have to ask, "How much is faith a part of me? How much does my faith affect who I am? Do my kids recognize the role that faith plays in my life?"

Our kids are beneficiaries of our obedience to God. They are the result of our trust in God. And they are witnesses to God's love through our example as we follow Him. Tamar, Rahab, and Ruth showed us the way.

While we are not responsible for our children's salvation—our children will not be saved through us; that's in God's hands—we have an opportunity to lay a foundation for our children. We are blessed with the authority to teach them about God. They are going to mess up. Many of our kids will stray from the path at some point. Hopefully, by then they will have a handy-dandy map in their pocket that will point them back in the direction of home.

Naomi returned home and brought with her a woman who would change the course of her history—and ours—simply by showing kindness. Sacrificial love, as we saw in Ruth, necessitates humility and requires us to put the needs of others over our own.

What does that mean for us? Pray that the Holy Spirit will empower you as you serve your family joyfully—even through laundry, dishes, and carpool. Pray that He will open your eyes to see ways to serve your husband, children, and those around you to make them feel loved and adored in a way that reflects the love of our Father in heaven. And pray that as you follow God, your children will follow in your footsteps to do the same.

FAITH AT HOME
COUNTING GOD'S PROMISES

Make a list of all the things we can count on every single day (the sun coming up, flowers blooming, birds chirping, etc.). Make a paper chain and write each promise on a link. Thank Him for all of His blessings.

> As surely as the sun rises,
> he will appear;
> he will come to us like the winter rains,
> like the spring rains that water the earth.
> Hosea 6:3

live out your faith

Blessed is the one who perseveres under trial because, having stood the test, that person will receive the crown of life that the Lord has promised to those who love him.
James 1:12

CHAPTER 13

A TRUSTED VOICE

When he was 18 months old, my middle son was helping me fill the front-loading washing machine. I took a few steps outside the laundry room and perched myself nearby with my camera in hand to record a video of this momentous occasion. I handed laundry duty over to my toddler.

After he struggled to close the door, I cheered, praised his helpfulness, and kept the camera rolling to see his reaction. Something shiny caught his eye: the silver bowl of dog food.

The cartoon angel and devil popped onto his shoulders as I saw him wrestle with temptation. I knew he wanted to eat a handful (or five) of those crunchy brown nuggets. His eyes stared unblinkingly at the bowl, aware, but not caring that I was watching (and videoing) him.

Every time he squatted down to touch the food, I said, "No, no," and he stood up abruptly. He remained laser-focused. Up and down and up and down. He responded to my voice each time. Down once more, I threw in the double name and my voice grew stern, "John Leyson, don't touch." He stood back up again. He looked at me, then at the food, then at me. And then his gaze shifted away toward something new.

I praised him again, "Thank you for listeni—" I didn't get to finish my sentence before he slammed the door in my face. He was going to get that dog food, alright, and he didn't want me to watch.

Age certainly plays a role in my reaction to disobedience. If my teenager slammed his door in my face, well, I would have had to cut the video short. There would have been words, a consequence, and *the look*.

Instead, I took my toddler by the hand and led him into the kitchen to eat food for humans. We kept the door to the laundry room closed so he wouldn't have access to the dog food anymore.

Sin from such an early age is indicative of the fallen world. By the time they reach the age of two, disobedience isn't so cute anymore. As they mature, their sins give us gray hair and keep us up at night.

And when we sin, those effects ripple down to those closest to us. It tears marriages apart. It wreaks havoc on even the strongest of family units. It's what causes bitterness that pits us against our husbands, secrets that devour trust, and self-indulging habits that create strongholds over what matters most.

The hardest part is the suffering we endure here on Earth. The worst part? So many never find their way to Jesus and spend an eternity separated from God.

Eve

In the beginning, God created and saw that it was good. Everything He created was good. Everything He creates to this day is good. Once He created people, everything was still good—perfect, in fact—until we opened the door to sin.

I recently saw a meme that said, "If Eve was from South Louisiana, she wouldn't have eaten the apple—she would have eaten the snake." It's true, y'all. We eat a lot of crazy things here. Maybe if Eve had been Cajun, she'd have avoided the fruit in the first place.

The very first mother, Eve, birthed sin in the easiest and most common way—through direct disobedience to God. She chose to listen to the serpent's voice instead of God's. Instantly she experienced fear, shame, and guilt—emotions that were never intended to be part of our nature, but were released immediately with the introduction of sin into God's perfection.

Then the man and his wife heard the sound of the LORD God as he was walking in the garden in the cool of the day, and they hid from the LORD God among the trees of the garden.
Genesis 3:8

Adam and Eve tried to run from God because they knew what they had done was wrong. Shame washed over them. Running was easier than coming face to face with their Creator and acknowledging their disobedience.

My kids also run from me when they know they've done something wrong. Running, hiding, and lying are their ways of protecting themselves from my disapproval. But hiding only delays the inevitable. Ultimately it puts them at risk of becoming more entangled in sin. And isn't it amazing that they don't realize I already know what they did? God probably thought the same about Adam and Eve.

So the LORD God banished him from the Garden of Eden...
Genesis 3:23

Within the first three chapters of the Bible, the whole world had both been created and destroyed. We'd been banished from the perfect home He created for us.

Sin wasn't inevitable. It was humanity's choice, with inescapable consequences. And yet, our story doesn't end in sin. It is lavished in love.

After Adam and Eve's sin, God clothed them (Genesis 3:21). He blessed them with the first two children to come from the womb of a mother.

Adam lay with his wife Eve, and she became pregnant and gave birth to Cain. She said, "With the help of the Lord I have brought forth a man." Later, she gave birth to his brother Abel.
Genesis 4:1-2

Bathsheba

In the spring, at the time when kings go off to war, David sent Joab out with the king's men and the whole Israelite army. They destroyed the Ammonites and besieged Rabbah. But David remained in Jerusalem. One evening David got up from his bed and walked around on the roof of the palace. From the roof he saw a woman bathing. The woman was very beautiful, and David sent someone to find out about her. The man said, "She is Bathsheba, the daughter of Eliam and the wife of Uriah the Hittite."
2 Samuel 11:1-3

Bathsheba was the granddaughter of David's counselor, Ahithophel the Gilonite, and daughter and wife of high-ranking warriors in the king's army. The men are listed among David's mighty warriors (2 Samuel 23:34 and 39). There were 37 men with this distinction. These honored men were on the front lines to protect him and his kingdom.

Because of his status, Uriah and Bathsheba's home was nestled close to the palace.

King David had risen from his comfy bed while his army was off at war. He took notice of the beautiful woman from his rooftop when she was bathing.

David was home in his palace instead of with his army on the battlefield. Already he wasn't where he was supposed to be physically—and spiritually. His heart strayed from God as he inquired about the beautiful woman he saw from his rooftop.

Despite knowing her father and husband, David sent messengers to summon Bathsheba. And that was only the beginning of this tragic story.

> *If a man commits adultery with another man's wife—with the wife of his neighbor—both the adulterer and the adulteress are to be put to death.*
> Leviticus 20:10.

Bathsheba walked away from her encounter with the king with the weight of a sin punishable by death at the time. She was entangled in the repercussions of David's sin. Sin doesn't just pull us down—it also pulls down the people around us. Gossip, slander, lies, lust, pride, and anger have a ripple effect on those around us.

In the events that followed, David broke the sixth, seventh, and tenth commandments: Bathsheba was pregnant with his son (2 Samuel 11:5); David tried to pin it on her husband (v. 6-13); David plotted Uriah's death (v. 14-24); David married Bathsheba (v. 27).

When Uriah's wife heard that her husband was dead, she mourned for him. After the time of mourning was over, David had her brought to his house, and she became his wife and bore him a son. But the thing David had done displeased the LORD.
2 Samuel 11:26-27

David was the king of Israel and became Bathsheba's husband. He was also the spiritual leader of God's kingdom and the spiritual leader of his household—but he was deeply entwined in sin. This sin had a devastating effect on Bathsheba's life and his kingdom.

A Faithful Advisor to the Rescue

God often places people in our lives who will guide us back to Him by telling us what we can't see. A beautiful example of this is when He sent the prophet Nathan to confront David. Through a parable that paralleled his story, David was quick to recognize the character's sin. But it took Nathan's guidance for him to be able to make the connection to his own choices.

Only a trusted mentor and friend can speak bold truths that will spur conviction that's not perceived as condemnation. Nathan's God-ordained wisdom brought David to confession before God. His words were a wake-up call for David. The prophet's guidance would be a turning point in Bathsheba's life on more than one occasion. Later in 1 Kings, Nathan's advice to Bathsheba became a turning point for the kingdom and Solomon's reign.

> *"Now then, let me advise you how you can save your own life and the life of your son Solomon."*
> 1 Kings 1:12

Divine guidance isn't always going to come in the form of a pillar of cloud or fire (Exodus 13:21-22). We typically won't get visits from angels like Hagar did in the desert. God uses the people around us to speak truths in our lives. Sometimes it takes the wise word of a mentor, friend, spouse, or leader to guide us to the right path. The Holy Spirit gifts us with discernment to take this wisdom to heart.

As our kids grow older, we are no longer the only voices who advise them to make wise decisions. I often pray for God to bring a Nathan to my children as their choices now have the potential to have larger consequences.

My preteen got a lunch detention for rocking back and forth in his chair after being told repeatedly to stop. After school, he mentioned it to his older brother and asked if he should tell me. His flesh wanted to hide this from me. James reminded him that lying was far worse a crime in our house than getting a detention. He confessed. I was so proud of him for telling me right away, but sensed his reluctance. I reminded him that though I'm not omniscient like God, there would be an email waiting in my inbox.

He did the right thing. I would have known anyway, but his confession is what made me draw him into a mama bear hug.

He still had detention, but thanks to his brother's guidance, he didn't face punishment at home, too. Had he lied, there would have been a much different outcome.

We have many voices speaking into our families. Of course, we hope we're always the ones our husbands and children will come to, but often it's someone else. Whose voice will our children listen to: the serpent's or God's? Whose voice will we listen to as mothers?

Nathan's truth-filled words helped not just David, but Bathsheba as well. His wisdom had an eternal consequence on their family. I'm grateful for the Nathans in our family's lives. They graciously point out when we are not living out our faith in accordance to God's Word.

> Then David said to Nathan, "I have sinned against the Lord."
> Nathan replied, "The Lord has taken away your sin."
> 2 Samuel 12:13

This was the turning point for their new family. But while there was good news for their eternal lives as David was freed from the bondage of sin, God did not change the outcome of His judgment on him. Bathsheba, too, would carry that grief for the rest of her earthly life until she held him in heaven. Thank God for eternity.

Heavenly Father, thank You for the people in my life who speak truth and offer wise counsel. Please continue to bless our family with others who will keep us on the right path. Help us turn away from sin to be free from its clutches. Though we don't deserve it, we are grateful You have taken our sins away. Just as You have used others to speak into my life, Lord, use me to pour into others with Your truth. May Your light be seen in me. In Christ's name. Amen.

F A I T H   A T   H O M E

T E L E P H O N E

Sit in a circle. Choose a phrase, affirmation, or short Bible verse and whisper it into the ear of the person next to you, who whispers it to the next person, and on and on. The last person to receive the message has to say it out loud. This activity emphasizes sharing accurate information and making sure what we share is true.

Then choose a silly untruth—nothing to hurt someone's feelings. For example: "Mom has a porcupine living in her closet." You can also discuss how lies and untruths spread easily but can be hurtful.

With the tongue we praise our Lord and Father, and with it we curse human beings, who have been made in God's likeness.
James 3:9

CHAPTER 14

SURVIVING SORROW

My mom struggled with alcoholism throughout my late teen years and early twenties. It was her way of coping with early life trauma, depression, grief, and stress that reached a climax when she hit menopause. Navigating the day-to-day was too difficult so she found an escape. She spent many of my college years in and out of rehab fighting to get sober.

I'd love to say that I handled her addiction with grace, but bitterness was at the helm of our relationship for years.

I wonder if Bathsheba felt the same toward David? How did she manage her grief? What was her response to trauma? And how did she balance the physical and emotional demands of raising a child while carrying the weight of the past on her shoulders?

We often fight our hardest battles because of the actions of those within our closest circles. Sometimes within our own homes.

Redemption and Restoration

Sitting on the edge of my mom's hospice bed, she shared her testimony with me—the moment she first met Jesus. It was after Dad passed away, at a time when she had hit rock bottom. Crying out to God from under a tree, she saw a vision. In it, rain poured from the sky and an umbrella shielded her from the downpour. But soon the floodwaters rose over her head and she couldn't breathe—until a Hand extended toward her. She grabbed hold of it. This Hand offered freedom. It offered life. God pulled her from the depths and she breathed fresh air for the first time in years. She saw the colors of nature—more vibrant than she had seen before. Her joy returned, and with it laughter, fun, dancing, silliness, and peace.

When she finished telling me she asked, "Did you write all that down? You need to share it." *I got it down, Mom.*

This testimony is her legacy. Her mother's prayers, and her daughters', were finally answered. She celebrated 14 years of sobriety, restored relationships, the birth of seven grandkids, and a life with Jesus before she met Him face to face.

But now, this is what the Lord says..."Do not fear, for I have redeemed you; I have summoned you by name; you are mine. When you pass through the waters, I will be with you; and when you pass through the rivers, they will not sweep over you. When you walk through the fire, you will not be burned; the flames will

not set you ablaze. For I am the Lord your God, the Holy One of Israel, your Savior..."
Isaiah 43:1-3

Bathsheba suffered through many traumas in her early life with David. An unwanted affair, the death of her husband, a new marriage a week later, her child's sudden illness, an absentee husband, and the death of her child.

Only after their child died, and after he had dinner (2 Samuel 12:20), did David comfort his wife. Bathsheba finally got to meet the godly side of King David.

Transformation is God's specialty.

"In the same way I will not cause pain without allowing something new to be born," says the Lord.
Psalm 66:9 ICB

Rebirth is His spoken promises fulfilled. God cultivates scorched terrain to make it fertile. From the flood to the rainbow, from slavery to freedom, from lost to found, from the desert to a kingdom, from the valley to the mountain tops, from the cross to the resurrection: God leads us on a journey to restoration. He lifts us from the depths and sets us back on solid ground.

Bathsheba witnessed a transformation in her husband and was gifted a son who would one day be king. She had a front-row seat to

God's goodness and love extended to His children, but that didn't come without first experiencing the terrors of the fallen world.

Life after Loss

My mom had a miscarriage early in her marriage to my dad. After they found out, she and my dad drove to the neighboring city of New Orleans with a camera and black and white film in hand. Together, they took snapshots around the city to document the solemn day.

Of all the pictures stored in our family photo albums from over the years, those are the only ones not in color. Now water-stained from hurricanes and floods, it's as if they captured the tears from such heartbreak. Mourning lasted beyond a day, just like the photographs last beyond memories.

A few months after she miscarried, my mom found out she was pregnant again. This time she would give birth nine months later to her rainbow baby—me.

God loved Bathsheba's sons. Both of them. God knows each of His children, even the ones we carry for just a short time here on this earth. His love is a greater love than we can ever fathom. We get a small glimpse of that love as we hold our children in our wombs and arms.

For those of you who have experienced the loss of a child, that scope broadens with the assurance that your children are safe in the arms of our Father. The breadth of his love extends beyond our short time on Earth. One day you, dear daughter of God, will hold them again.

"Can I bring him back again? I will go to him, but he will not return to me."
Then David comforted his wife Bathsheba...
2 Samuel 12:24

Life after loss is never the same. Our still-beating hearts yearn for a future with our loved ones who are no longer with us. It can be hollowing. And life doesn't pause for us to heal. We still have to adult, tend to our home and other children, go to work, walk the dog, and on and on. But it's in these periods of grief when we see Jesus more clearly. He joined in the world's suffering from His conception in the womb. He took our place on the cross. He grieved for us and with us. His resurrection brings hope in our seasons of deep loss.

I give them eternal life, and they shall never perish; no one will snatch them out of my hand. My Father, who has given them to me, is greater than all; no one can snatch them out of my Father's hand. I and the Father are one.
John 10:28-30

To those of us who know God, the loss of a loved one gives us an eternal mindset. We know that Earth is not our eternal home. One day, there will be a joyous reunion.

In our sorrow, we're reminded there is more to come. We grow in empathy, love, and patience. Our hearts become tender toward those experiencing similar hurts. We have the blessed opportunity to then join God in their healing through prayer, fellowship, and mentorship.

When grief is fresh, we can't imagine going forward without our loved ones. In time, the pain subsides and we feel God's peace laced within the tapestry of grief. Healing begins as He mends our hurts and transforms our hearts.

Hope returns as we live out our faith. For my mom, it was the birth of her daughters, and after another wave of trials, restored relationships with us.

For Bathsheba, God redeemed a marriage and continued to fulfill His promise to Abraham with the birth of Solomon. Though there continued to be trials during David's reign, Bathsheba, Solomon, and God's people experienced a period of peace with the rise of Solomon as king.

Their story is full of heartbreak, but it is not without hope. In fact, the Hope of the world stems from their family tree. Along with Tamar, Rahab, and Ruth, Bathsheba is listed as one of Jesus' maternal ancestors in chapter one of the book of Matthew.

*She gave birth to a son, and they named him Solomon. The Lord
loved him; and because the Lord loved him, he sent word through
Nathan the prophet to name him Jedidiah.*
2 Samuel 12:24-25

As we learned in Jochebed's story, God knows us all by name.
He doesn't necessarily call us by the name on our birth certificates—
though He knows that, too—but He knows who we are within our
hearts.

He names the baby *Jedidiah* which means "loved by the Lord."
And though we aren't told the name of Bathsheba's first son, God
knows that too. What a great reminder to a family who had lost so
much.

David told his son about his message from the Lord:

*But you will have a son who will be a man of peace and rest, and I
will give him rest from all his enemies on every side. His name
will be Solomon, and I will grant Israel peace and quiet during his
reign. He is the one who will build a house for my Name. He will
be my son, and I will establish the throne of his kingdom over
Israel forever.*
1 Chronicles 22:9-10

Who else has the authority to gift peace, quiet, and rest but the
Great Commander Himself? Rest is the root of restoration. Biblical

restoration means to not only be restored to where you once were but to receive more than what was lost. The new version is made better than the old one. While much of David's reign was spent on the battlefield, growth, prosperity, and an eternal legacy were birthed from a period of peace during the reign of King Solomon. Bathsheba was at both of their sides during these periods of trials and triumphs.

God breathed creation and restoration into the lives of sinful beings. He doesn't want separation; he wants reconciliation. He restores our broken spirits, relationships, and homes for generations to come.

> *But from everlasting to everlasting*
> *the Lord's love is with those who fear him,*
> *and his righteousness with their children's children—*
> *with those who keep his covenant*
> *and remember to obey his precepts.*
> Psalm 103:17-18

You, blessed mama, are carrying around plenty of burdens. Some may be the result of your sin, others may be the repercussions of another's, and the rest are because we live in a fallen and broken world. Perhaps it's grief, perhaps it's suffering in another form, but God...

He has the ability to free you from those burdens and He

desires to do so. Out of seasons of hardship come seasons of peace and rest.

No matter the type of suffering we are experiencing, God welcomes us into his stress-management system. We can become overwhelmed by grief or hardships until we allow God in to help us. We tend to choose for ourselves what we carry around with us. It shapes our relationships, our decisions, our actions, and our reactions.

What if we asked God which burdens we were meant to carry? We tend to put a lot on ourselves. We continue to carry the weight of the world when God never intended for us to do so. Instead, He offers to remove them completely from our shoulders.

> I heard an unknown voice say,
> "Now I will take the load from your shoulders;
> I will free your hands from their heavy tasks.
> You cried to me in trouble, and I saved you..."
> Psalm 81:5-7 NLT

Other times, He shoulders those burdens himself to shield us from the weight.

> Praise be to the Lord, to God our Savior, who daily bears our burdens.
> Psalm 68:19

But some burdens, such as grief, He comes alongside us as we carry them.

We still navigate hard times, but Jesus lightens the load. He invites us to be yoked to Him—side by side with our Savior.

Then Jesus said, "Come to me, all of you who are weary and carry heavy burdens, and I will give you rest. Take my yoke upon you. Let me teach you, because I am humble and gentle at heart, and you will find rest for your souls. For my yoke is easy to bear, and the burden I give you is light."
Matthew 11:28-30

If you are walking in grief, God can bring comfort and peace to your heart. He walks with us and keeps us from being crushed. I've prayed for your healing.

May God wrap His loving arms around you in your time of need. May the promise of heaven give you hope of a beautiful reunion one day.

"So with you, Now is your time of grief, but I will see you again and you will rejoice, and no one will take away your joy."
John 16:22

FAITH AT HOME

TALENT SHOW

Let your kids show off their different skills and talents with a family talent show. God gave them each unique abilities and passions that He wants you to help foster in them as they grow to know Him more. Help the kids brainstorm what they can show off. Do your kids enjoy singing, acting, dancing, tumbling, or stand-up comedy? Create a "stage" for them to perform. Some skills such as painting, sculpting, writing poetry, or building Lego® designs may take some prep time. Allow the kids to present their works of art from the stage. Afterward, have everyone join you on stage for a worship dance party!

Each of you should use whatever gift you have received to serve others, as faithful stewards of God's grace in its various forms.
1 Peter 4:10

CHAPTER 15

SHIFTING ROLES

Whose bright idea was it to hand a three-year-old a metal bat? And why did I agree to coach tee-ball? I had spent the past hour teaching preschoolers how to hit a baseball. From behind, I positioned their feet by the plate and their hands on the bat. "Okay, now look at the ball and freeze." This part was for my own safety as I quickly, and without taking my eyes off the batter, took three steps backward. "Now swing and don't let go of the bat." That last part was also for my safety. "Gently…I said gently…put the bat down and run that way to first base! Go! Go! Go!"

Coaching toddlers was like herding feral kittens. When they weren't at bat, the rest of the team stood in a huddle in the infield, dog piling on top of the ball anytime a batter hit it more than a few inches off the tee. Many of the batters followed their ball into the field to get to it before the other players.

Multiple batters ran in the wrong direction toward third base. Or across the pitcher's mound to second. Or to their parents. Several heaved the bat in my direction before hustling to first. When it was John Leyson's turn, he stood there watching the ball fly into the air. I side-skipped along the baseline, waving my hands, urging him toward me until he tagged first base and gave me a high-five.

I held a brief parent meeting at the end of practice. As I was going over the ballpark rules and practice schedule, my son decided he was done. Like, *done* done. It was hot and humid, past dinner time, nearing bedtime—the witching hour. Because I did not pick him up immediately, he attempted to climb up me. And by climb, I mean he grabbed onto my athletic shorts, pulled, and pantsed me in front of all the parents. That was the last time I wore shorts without a drawstring or belt.

Slowly but surely, we all got the hang of it. For John Leyson's first game, I no longer needed to position his hands and feet. He knew just what to do. I stepped back, spoke words of encouragement, and watched him swing. As the ball flew in the air, I cheered for him to run the bases. I was right there at home plate with my arms outstretched to embrace John Leyson when he scored his first run.

Over the years my role transitioned from coach to cheerleader. I now sit on the sidelines, but I have the best view.

When my littlest baby entered the school years, I felt the shift of a new era in our home. No more nursing, no more diapers, no more spoon-feeding or burping. They no longer need me to take care of their physical wellness. Unless they're sick. And even then, they no longer want me to fuss over them. I get a thrill every time my kids reach for my hand because soon holding Mommy's hand won't be cool. I already feel the slight tug of resistance when I squeeze a little tighter so they can't let go.

My three not-so-little loves are too big for my lap now, so I have to extend my arms around them to snuggle as we sit side-by-side. After being their world for so long (and them being mine), it's hard to let them grow up.

Advocating for Our Children

The queens in the Old Testament lived a life of royalty but were highly oppressed. In the book of Esther, the Persian Queen Vashti was exiled for not coming when the king demanded.

Then, the king's new bride, Queen Esther, risked being put to death when she approached the king without an invitation to do so.

Spoiler alert if you are not familiar with her story: she saved the Jewish people from execution and became a hero to her people. Her favor with the king, her husband, was not typical or consistent with his past behavior.

Her advocacy was a risk.

Bathsheba lived a vastly different lifestyle from these two queens. She was a diplomat in King David's court and the king respected her as such. His relationship with her was unique compared to other kings and queens.

The two grew old together and David's body became frail. One of David's sons, Adonijah, took advantage of the ailing king and claimed the throne for himself. The prophet, Nathan, knowing that this was not what God or David desired, reached out to help Bathsheba whose life and the life of her son Solomon were in danger. Adonijah, David's older son, would have surely destroyed anyone who would threaten his place on the throne.

Bathsheba, fearing for her life, needed to let David know what was happening. As she approached her husband's bedside, she bowed down before him (1 Kings 1:16).

She reminded him that he had named Solomon as his successor and gave him the news of what was happening in his kingdom. By doing so, she fought righteously for her son to arise to his place on the throne. The title wasn't hers to give, but she took the matter to the king and bowed before him.

Bathsheba's advocacy for her son not only saved his life but led him to the role God had intended for him. She interceded for her son before the king just as we do when we kneel before our Father on behalf of our children.

Our intuition is God-given. Those checks in our mama-guts are often discernments from Him. God gives us the confidence to be their voice. We know when our children are not well so we advocate for their health. We know when they deserve more and we fight for access to a good education. When a kid on the playground says something mean to our child, we get feisty and...well, no, the Holy Spirit holds us back on that one.

In 1 Kings 1:22, the prophet, Nathan, arrived to echo Bathsheba's claims and hear the king's wishes. When Bathsheba was invited back into the king's bedroom, her posture was different as David addressed her.

So she came into the king's presence and stood before him.
1 Kings 1:28

Mamas, we are invited into the presence of the King, to stand before Him on behalf of our children. He hears our cries, His eyes rest on our tear-stained faces, and He holds our hands in His.

God hears our prayers and answers them according to His will. Nothing is beyond His abilities.

A friend of mine has three teenage girls who are the sweetest, most respectful, and most joyful teens I've ever met. She and her husband have a great relationship with them.

It appeared she hadn't faced the terror of teenage girls that everyone talks about.

I asked her, "What's your secret?"

And she simply said, "I prayed against it. I said it wasn't going to happen."

She advocated for her child before God. She and her husband

prayed for their parent/child relationships into adulthood. I'm praying this over my children and over me as well.

When Bathsheba met with David, God's promise was fulfilled once again (1 Chronicles 22:6-10): the throne would be established through Solomon's line.

David then swore an oath from his deathbed that Solomon would become king. With this oath, Solomon usurped his brother and took his God-appointed seat on the throne.

God had favor on this ancestral line from the beginning.

> *The days are coming,' declares the Lord,*
> *'when I will raise up for David a righteous Branch,*
> *a King who will reign wisely*
> *and do what is just and right in the land...*
> *This is the name by which he will be called:*
> *The Lord Our Righteous Savior.*
> Jeremiah 23:5-6

God used Bathsheba to fulfill His promise. Her role had an eternal impact on all future generations.

From Advocating to Advising

When Solomon became king, Bathsheba's role within the court shifted from being the wife of the king to the mother of the king.

When Bathsheba went to King Solomon to speak to him for Adonijah, the king stood up to meet her, bowed down to her and sat down on his throne. He had a throne brought for the king's mother, and she sat down at his right hand.

1 Kings 2:19

When the crown passed from David to Solomon, Bathsheba took on a prestigious role as queen mother beside her son. His posture of humility as he stood and bowed before her—an act that was typically reserved for him—shows his love, dedication, and respect he has for his mother.

The throne set beside his placed her in a position of honor as a trusted advisor and counselor to him.

As our children grow older, our role shifts as they gain the ability to make decisions and speak for themselves. We are no longer their advocates. Instead, we become their advisors and wise counsel. We shift from head coach to first base coach as we steer them in the right direction.

In fourth grade, my oldest son smoothly slipped the phrase "my girlfriend" into a conversation. He quickly added, "I know, I know... I'm not allowed to kiss or hold hands until college."

Phew! "So what does a fourth-grade romance look like?" I asked him.

He responded, "Well, we play tag on the playground."

Oh. Okay. I played it way cool. I pray he will want to come to me when his feelings for girls go beyond playing tag. You know, like, in a decade.

More recently, before the words "I told you so" could escape my lips, he announced: "Note to my future self: Mom is always right." I told him I was going to write that down—publish it in a book—for when he forgets. He's learned a few lessons the hard way and is starting to trust my wisdom a little more. Selective trust, that is.

I hope he'll continue to turn to me when he needs a listening ear. I want him to feel comfortable approaching me with whatever is going on in his little world. He won't always like what I have to say, but I continue to ask him, "Has there ever been a time when I've said 'no' just to be mean?"

He has yet to think of one. Because I am on his team. His coach. I want the best for him and will champion him, while also lovingly guiding him toward the right path. Like the wise wizard, Gandalf, famously spoke in *Lord of the Rings*, "Bilbo Baggins... I am not trying to rob you, I'm trying to help you." Ah, wee hobbits still have a lot to learn.

As my kids grow into grizzly bear-like teenagers with opinions and hormones, I pray that they listen and consider what I say. I hope they always respect me enough to turn to me for guidance and see *me* as a listening ear whom they can count on to always speak truth and love to them.

Here's a bit of hard truth: I don't always deserve their respect. The times I have spoken too harshly or blown up over something insignificant are too numerous to count. If I don't put myself in check, they won't see me as the type of mom they can come to for mentorship.

Our kids are immersed in our home culture. The language we use toward our spouses and children will be reflected in the way our children communicate with the world. They pick up subtle nuances in our demeanors. They learn about building relationships by watching us navigate ours. Kids learn to trust their parents as we help them make good choices. They eventually learn that we do know a thing or two.

Even after Solomon became king, he sought his mom's advice before making decisions for his kingdom. He didn't always take it (and we can't expect our kids to do the same), but he held esteem for her wisdom. He knew she wanted the best for him. Perhaps when our kids are grown, they'll still save a seat for us mamas next to them from time to time.

God has His hand on your family as well. As you are invited before the throne to advocate for your child, what can you bring to Him right now? What has you worried or stressed? Has your role shifted to that of an advisor? Pray that God gifts you with the right words to share with your child. Pray for Him to be at the center of your parent-to-child relationships. As you pray over your relationships, pray against the norm. Don't let the terrible twos or the terrifying teen years, natural tendencies, or the pull of the world's disrespectful indoctrination define your children and your relationship with them. May these years be filled with love, joy, and mutual respect with Jesus at the center. Christ-centered parenting is how we live out our faith.

FAITH AT HOME

DRESSING FOR WINTER

Give your kids a white shirt to wear. Then, tell them to put on as many shirts, jackets, scarves, etc. they can fit. Once the layers start to get uncomfortable and heavy, talk about how sins weigh us down and keep us from moving freely on our walks with Christ. Now, have them take off one item of clothing at a time, naming each one as sin. Jesus takes off our sins and forgives us. When you get to the white shirt, discuss how Jesus washes us white as snow.

"Come now, let us settle the matter," says the LORD. "Though your sins are like scarlet, they shall be as white as snow; though they are red as crimson, they shall be like wool."
Isaiah 1:18

F R O M   S T R E N G T H   T O   S T R E N G T H

6:00 a.m. – My alarm goes off, but no worries, I am already awake because my middle child has his internal alarm set to 5:30 a.m.

6:05 a.m.—I run to take a shower and take advantage of this quiet time by staring at the wall.

6:20 a.m.—I'm trying to convince myself that I should get out of the shower to wake the others.

6:27 a.m.—Still trying to convince myself.

6:30 a.m.—My second alarm goes off and oh, no! I haven't gotten out of the shower to dry my hair or put makeup on for the day. Oh yeah, and get dressed.

6:32 a.m.—Dressed at least, I shake the kids awake, flicking on lights, making as much noise as I can, and singing obnoxious songs to raise my oldest and youngest from their drool-filled slumbers.

6:45 a.m.—Whoa, where did the time go? Up and at 'em!

6:48 a.m.—By now, I start raising my voice for my kids to get out of bed and get dressed.

7:00 a.m.—The boys are dressed in their uniforms. One of them can't find his belt. Baby Girl is staring at the wall. She gets it from her mama.

7:05 a.m.—Everyone is on the hunt for the missing belt.

7:08 a.m.—Kids make breakfast (Pop-Tarts®) while Mom is left to find the belt.

7:15 a.m.—Third alarm goes off. Kids shove Pop-Tarts® in their mouths and go brush their teeth.

7:18 a.m.—Kids grab their backpacks and head to the door.

7:20 a.m.—Fourth alarm goes off. Middle child doesn't have socks or shoes on. Forgot to dress Baby Girl.

7:25 a.m.—The middle child's shoes are officially missing. Baby Girl is trying to shove her head through the armhole, pants are on backward, shoes—hers are missing as well.

7:30 a.m.—Where are the shoes? Mom is tearing apart the bedrooms, oldest is searching outside and in the car, middle one is in the living room crying because we're going to be late for school, and Baby Girl decided to stop getting dressed to play with toys.

7:35 a.m. on the dot—The shoes magically appear. Praise Jesus!

7:36 a.m.—Everyone loads up in the car. I run back inside because I forgot keys, purse, and someone else forgot his lunch.

7:58 a.m.—Last car in carpool line. Welcome to the life of a mom.

And this was a day when we didn't have any kids fighting or tantrums or bathroom floods because my daughter plugged the sink up with toilet paper again. I'm usually ready for my nap by 8:30 a.m.

Strength. Without it, I wouldn't be able to make it through the day.

My daily stressors have a stronghold on me. When they overwhelm me, I write them down to view them from another perspective. These "annoyances" aren't as menacing on paper. Trivial, even. Every one of them. Why would I allow them to control my mood and give them the power to drain my strength? The days like I described above all have one thing in common: they begin with me staring at the wall, instead of kneeling before God.

What did these mothers in the Bible stress out about? Tamar was concerned about being able to have legitimate children through Judah's line. Rahab knew of the impending destruction of Jericho—her home—and feared for her safety and that of her family. Ruth was the sole caretaker of her mother-in-law and had to find ways to provide for them in a foreign land. After these huge, stressful times for each of them, perhaps motherhood seemed like a walk in the park by comparison.

Finding Strength in God

When I read about Bathsheba, I imagine her to have strength, poise, beauty, and grace—Mrs. Israel 986 BC. There's a theory that

Proverbs 31 was written by King Solomon (using the pen name, King Lemuel) about his mother, Bathsheba. There's no proof to that theory, but I love envisioning Bathsheba in verses 10 through 31.

I wonder if the women in the Bible looked anything like I imagine them? Imagining their physical features reminds me that they were real people—mothers—who thousands of years later are remembered for their faith.

Bathsheba suffered through a forced affair, the death of her husband, the illness and death of her first child, her and Solomon's life on the line while Adonijah was king, a lot of drama from David's other sons, their entire household fleeing to the Mount of Olives to escape a threat to the kingdom (2 Samuel 15), and the death of her second husband and king.

Suddenly my morning routine doesn't look so bad.

But whether we struggle with keeping up with the day-to-day or facing a larger-than-life reality, motherhood brings out something fierce in us women. We fight for the lives of our children but are powerless without God's strength.

It is because of motherhood that I learned what it means to fully depend on God to carry me through the day.

Arise, cry out in the night,
as the watches of the night begin;
pour out your heart like water
in the presence of the Lord.

Lift up your hands to him
for the lives of your children,
who faint from hunger
at every street corner.
Lamentations 2:19

Since becoming a mom, I frequently return to these heartbreaking verses. Literally, children were dying in the streets because the people of Israel had turned their backs on God. Spiritually, this is what happens to our children when they fall away from Him. These mothers were crying out to God—with untamed ferocity and blazing fervency.

These verses are a reminder of the urgency and importance to pray for our children. There's a vicious enemy on the prowl.

Sometimes I don't have words for God. What pours out of my heart is a simple, "Jesus, help." When I don't know what I truly need, "Help!" is the only thing I can muster. Pouring out our hearts to God doesn't have to be lengthy and shouldn't be verbose (Matthew 6:7-8). It doesn't have to be filled with lofty or holy-sounding language or follow a checklist or a script. It is simply connecting with God—our hearts to his. When we don't have the words, we can always turn to Scripture and pray through David's prayers.

It is God who arms me with strength
and keeps my way secure.

He makes my feet like the feet of a deer;

he causes me to stand on the heights.

He trains my hands for battle;

my arms can bend a bow of bronze.

You make your saving help my shield;

your help has made me great.

You provide a broad path for my feet,

so that my ankles do not give way.

2 Samuel 22:33-37

Blessed are those whose strength is in you,

whose hearts are set on pilgrimage.

As they pass through the Valley of Baka,

they make it a place of springs;

the autumn rains also cover it with pools.

They go from strength to strength,

till each appears before God in Zion.

Psalm 84:5-7

The hidden meanings in these verses give them added significance when we look at their origins. *Baka* (or in some translations *Baca*) is another word for *tears* or *weeping*. Also, the Hebrew word for *pool*, in this instance, also means *blessing*.

If we walk through hardships (or valleys) drawing from the strength of God, asking Him to carry us across them, then the valleys will not be desolate. Instead, the landscape transforms into lush fields and babbling creeks.

An abundance of flowers and wildlife show signs of life in places that were once barren. God Himself paves the path ahead and marks it with blessings declaring the way forward as His territory. He carries us across the valley, from mountaintop to mountaintop, from "*strength to strength*" all the days of our lives.

We're often told, "God doesn't give you more than you can handle." But this phrase couldn't be further from the truth. He gives us more than we can handle without Him.

God does not select people He deems strongest and hand all of life's messes to them. He does not set aside a select few with superpowers and throw grenades at them.

He does not hand out hardships on a platter to those who carry medals of honor.

We *all* go through trials. And we can't handle them well alone. Instead of relying on our own, inadequate strength, when overwhelming hardships come, God reminds us to lean on Him.

Have I not commanded you? Be strong and courageous. Do not be afraid; do not be discouraged, for the Lord your God will be with you wherever you go.
Joshua 1:9

God carries us through valleys by His overcoming strength

when we allow Him to pick us up.

Whatever struggles we are going through right now in parenting, we can be assured it will not be like this forever. The sun rises anew for a fresh start every morning. Our kids won't be little for much longer. The laundry won't always be piled this high. Our kids do eventually learn to use the potty on their own. (I questioned this a few years back, but I have indeed witnessed this miracle.)

One day they will grow up and leave the comfort and protection of our homes to build their own. The day may come when we hand them off to a husband or wife. The mothers in the Bible bore witness to their children becoming adult men and women with families of their own.

...come out and look, you daughters of Zion. Look on King Solomon wearing a crown, the crown with which his mother crowned him on the day of his wedding, the day his heart rejoiced. Song of Songs 3:11

Take a minute to paint this picture across your mind: Bathsheba's heart swelling with love and pride as she placed the crown on Solomon's head. After years of caring for him, teaching him, shaping him, and guiding him, her job was done.

God carried her through the hard years to the crowning moment of fulfillment. Bathsheba stepped out of her role as Solomon stepped into his.

God's grace upon this family is the same grace He extends to you and me. His strength is the same that carries us through.

I received the following message from a fellow artist friend and want to bless you with these words today:

Sweet friend, Jesus' grace is sufficient to see you through your days. He has equipped you with His strength and determination. You are a powerful woman of God.

Pray for increased strength today, warrior moms. But *lean on* His. Ask God to carry you across the valley and make it a place of springs. If you are right now standing on a mountaintop, praise Him for the last valley He carried you through. Take some time and your current vantage point to look at all that He made beautiful in that valley. Worship Him now with songs of praise and fill your home with joy and gladness today.

FAITH AT HOME
DRIVE-BY PRAYERS

Pile everyone in the car and go for a drive. Choose random houses or drive to a friend's house. As you drive by, pray for that home and family. If you are friends with the family and know they wouldn't mind, use chalk to write in their driveway, "We prayed for you today." Drive by local businesses, churches, parks, and schools and pray over each of them.

> *I urge, then, first of all, that petitions, prayers, intercession and thanksgiving be made for all people—*
> 1 Timothy 2:1

serve the Lord

And Mary said:
"My soul glorifies the Lord and my spirit rejoices in God my Savior,
for he has been mindful of the humble state of his servant.
From now on all generations will call me blessed,
for the Mighty One has done great things for me—
holy is his name."
Luke 1:46-49

CHAPTER 17

THE NATIVITY

God's love, faithfulness, grace, and character are woven through the stories of Jochebed, Hagar, the Shunammite woman, Tamar, Rahab, Ruth, and Bathsheba, and continues throughout Mary's story. These mothers' stories, and many others, have been eternally sealed in Scripture to teach us truth, give us wisdom, and guide us as we live in a way that glorifies God.

From Genesis to Revelation, the beginning and the end have already been written. We know how it started and how it will finish. Sandwiched in the middle is the turning point of hope—the birth of Christ.

My middle son was born in mid-October, 2009. When Christmastime rolled around, he was two months old, content as could be, and a terrific sleeper: the perfect combination to play baby Jesus in the church musical.

I remember nursing him in the green room moments before the

curtain call, putting him in his "milk coma," swaddling him into an even deeper stupor, and handing him off to the actor playing Mary. Then I raced out to the audience to find my seat.

They could not have chosen a baby with a better disposition. He slept in "Mary's" arms during all of the rehearsals and two of the three performances. But during the third performance, he woke up when Mary started singing. I could see his big, beautiful, brown eyes looking up at her, but he still didn't make a sound. Later, the actor told me she fought back tears on stage as she looked back into his eyes. That moment when Mary first held her son—the Messiah— became so real to her. I felt it from the audience, too.

The Nativity, the visual representation of what is believed to be the scene of Jesus' birth, is widely marketed in many countries across the world during Christmas. It is seen in millions of homes every year, each depicted in slightly different ways.

Our family has four Nativity scenes. We have a clay set from Panama that's more glue than clay at this point. We also have one from Haiti in which the barn is represented by a hollowed-out coconut. In that set, there are at least twelve male figures. Surely one is Joseph, but He is indistinguishable from the rest.

Our Little People™ set has a few bite marks from dogs and toddlers, and because we bought a new set to replace some lost and chewed-up pieces from the original one, we have two Baby Jesuses. Our children insist that we use "Jesus' twin" and one-armed Mary as well.

Lastly, we have a Nativity scene that I painted on wood boards that sits by the entrance to our house. This one stays up year-round because we forget to put it away with the rest of the decorations after the holiday. But maybe that was God's idea all along—so the reminder of this important, faith-shaping event is a daily rather than annual reminder for our kids.

The birth of Jesus Christ is *the* pivotal moment in history, and yet, we often become desensitized to it. The Nativity has become merely another Christmas decoration. I want to always look upon the birth of Christ with overwhelming reverence.

I long for my heart to connect with that moment just as the woman who played Mary on stage while holding my son. Spend time today in awe of the moment of Jesus' birth. It deserves it.

Mary

> *Jacob the father of Joseph, the husband of Mary, of whom was born Jesus, who is called Christ.*
> Matthew 1:16

Throughout the Old Testament, hundreds of prophecies were made about the Messiah. These prophecies weren't vague but described in detail His unique and holy birth, ministry, death, and resurrection.

His arrival, especially, was not what one would have expected from God's arrival into the world.

> *Therefore the Lord himself will give you a sign: The virgin will*
> *conceive and give birth to a son, and will call him Immanuel.*
> Isaiah 7:14

Immanuel means "God with us." This prophecy, and all the others, was fulfilled. The Messiah was born as the Scriptures had said. While He was on earth, He performed miracles and offered His own prophecies about His second coming.

> *For as lightning that comes from the east is visible even in the*
> *west, so will be the coming of the Son of Man.*
> Matthew 24:27

When Jesus returns, it will not be in the humble form of a baby, the Bible tells us. He will appear in all His glory. As Christians, awaiting Jesus' second coming is fundamental to our beliefs. Just as we wait ever-so-patiently for that day, in their time, Mary, Joseph, and all of God's people were waiting for prophecies like Isaiah's to be fulfilled.

The angel Gabriel appeared to Mary to tell her news that would alter eternity. Being raised in the Jewish faith and learning from the teachings of the Old Testament, Mary would have known about Isaiah's prophecy. She would have grown up hearing the stories about Tamar, Rahab, Ruth, and Bathsheba.

Though Matthew listed each of these women in Jesus' genealogy through Joseph's lineage, Luke's account takes a different approach.

And Jacob the father of Joseph, the husband of Mary, and Mary was the mother of Jesus...
Matthew 1:16

[Jesus] was the son, so it was thought, of Joseph, the son of Heli,
Luke 3:23

Heli was Mary's father and Joseph's father-in-law through his marriage to Mary. Envision Mary piecing these facts together as she found out she, a granddaughter of David, betrothed to his great-great-great (and on and on) grandson, would join the list of women in the Messiah's family tree.

Can you imagine the truth dawning on Mary? *Am I THE virgin?* To Mary, it still didn't seem possible. She asked, *"How will this be... since I am a virgin?"* (Luke 1:34).

We often put our own boundaries on what God can do, but as Gabriel assured Mary, *"No word from God will ever fail"* (Luke 1:37). He made a virgin a mother. The fulfillment of His promises seems to be a common theme here.

For nothing will be impossible with God.
Luke 1:37 ESV

God uses us to fulfill His promises. He is not dependent on our obedience, but if He has called us for a specific purpose, it's time for us to follow that calling.

"I am the Lord's servant," Mary answered, "May your word to me be fulfilled."
Luke 1:38

Mary wasn't going to be birthing just any child, but the Lamb of God. Her calling as a mother went beyond the physical task of raising a child.

To enter servitude with God when raising our children means we bring them up in the way of the Lord. When we take on the role of motherhood, we are serving God as He intends us to raise His children.

I am the Lord's servant. This response will help us parent in a way that honors God.

It took a lot of love and commitment—and prompting from God—for Joseph to still marry Mary. Just as God chose Mary to carry His Son, He chose Joseph to be Jesus' earthly father. And he, like Mary, was faithfully obedient to God.

For generations, the Lord had played an active role in Joseph and Mary's family tree, planning for this very moment. Gabriel was sent once again to deliver big news—this time to a man who thought he would be ending his engagement.

I love that God sent an angel to calm the hearts of both Mary and Joseph. He tells them not to be afraid (Matthew 1:20 and Luke 1:30) and sets them both at ease.

Years ago, God pointed my husband and me toward a huge life change. I was surprised that I wasn't terrified at the thought. God gave both my husband and me peace about it. He didn't just tell me not to be afraid, or just my husband; He allowed peace to wash over both of us.

Joseph and Mary were living in Nazareth but were forced to return to Bethlehem for the mandatory census. The New Testament is far from the first time we've heard mention of this town.

> But you, Bethlehem Ephrathah,
> though you are small among the clans of Judah,
> out of you will come for me
> one who will be ruler over Israel,
> whose origins are from old,
> from ancient times.
> Micah 5:2

The significance of that particular town dates back generations. So many pieces had to fall into place for Joseph to return to his hometown (such as when Ruth and Naomi returned there from Moab). God set these plans in motion long before Naomi left Bethlehem in the first place, even before God divided the tribes of Israel. It had been prophesied that the Messiah would be born in that tiny blip on the map.

> *While they were there, the time came for the baby to be born, and she gave birth to her firstborn, a son. She wrapped him in cloths and placed him in a manger, because there was no guest room available for them.*
> Luke 2:6-7

A cry in the night. A baby cradled in a young mother's arms. A family away from home, weary from travel and childbirth. Mary and Joseph quietly celebrated this holy moment as the rest of the world was idly unaware.

Shepherds heralded by a heavenly host of angels, witnessed the glory of God before them, then rushed to meet the Messiah. No trumpets or balloons announced His arrival, but the shepherds spread the news, glorifying and praising God because what they saw was exactly what God told His people would happen.

His followers then told their children, and their children told their children.

The night would become one we would come to celebrate every year, with our carefully crafted nativity scenes being one of many things that we use to adorn our homes in observance.

Can I ask you a favor? Will you put down this book for a moment and open your Bible to Luke 2? Will you read this story out loud? No words of mine can do this moment justice, so I encourage you to read it today even if it isn't Christmastime. Especially if it isn't Christmastime.

I'll wait.

Luke's beautiful account of Christ's birth ushers in an era of hope and redemption. Matthew, Mark, Luke, and John recorded the events that happened over the course of Jesus' 33 years on earth—His birth, His ministry, His death, His resurrection, and all the miracles in between.

Finally, because of God's fulfillment of His promise to send us a Savior, Jesus inhabits the seat at the right hand of His Father in heaven. And His followers (that's us) are gifted an eternal home in His kingdom.

Mary, His mother, was the first to believe Jesus, the fruit of her womb, was the Christ.

Blessed is she who has believed that the Lord would fulfill his promises to her.
Luke 1:45

Now say this out loud: "*Blessed am I who have believed that the Lord would fulfill His promises to me.*"

The Lord has chosen you to raise the children He has given you, just as He chose Mary to raise His Son. Serve the Lord in this blessed role. He has a special plan for you and He has a special plan for each of your children. He believes in you, He has equipped you, and He will strengthen you on this journey of motherhood. Praise Him and give God the glory for all your parenting milestones.

FAITH AT HOME

NATIVITY

Take time to reflect on Jesus' birth and life. Send your kids on a scavenger hunt to find toys and items to create your own Nativity scene. For example, build a stable out of Lego® blocks, a tiny doll can be baby Jesus, Barbie can be Mary, etc. Or you can use playdough to mold all the people and animals. Be creative! Read Luke 2:1-21 together as a family.

CHAPTER 18

RAISING A CHILD OF GOD

Over the years, our conversations in MOMentum—a Bible study group for moms—often led to recounts of Godzilla-moments with our toddlers. You know, the ones when your child is wreaking havoc in the middle of aisle three at the grocery store.

Each of my children went through a stage when they would randomly fall to the ground, thrash, roll around, and shriek like banshees at decibel levels sure to cause hearing loss. Always in public. Always.

I still can't take my teen boys shopping without them having a wrestling match at Walmart. One mom recently said, "I'm convinced my two-year-old is going to grow up to be a sociopath." Having been there, we all laughed and nodded our heads.

Many times, I've looked at my children as they throw ridiculous tantrums, tell incredible lies, or put their sibling in a chokehold and think, "There is no way this child will grow up to be a functioning member of society."

When our worries and fears about our children's tantrums, bad attitudes, quirks, struggles, illnesses, and growing independence consume us, it's easy to forget that God is in control. We love to be behind the wheel, the one plotting our path, the one choosing the destination. And yet we are called to surrender it all to Him. We can trust God with the big stuff—and the little stuff—and continue to walk in His ways as we parent.

Hannah

God knew what He was doing when He chose Mary to be the mother of His Son. He needed a woman who was capable of completely surrendering her child to God. It had to be challenging for Mary who worried as all moms do (as we will see a little later). I wonder if she looked to Hannah's story in 1 Samuel 1 and 2 to encourage her along the way.

Like many women whose heart's desire is to be a mother, Hannah struggled with infertility for years. Perhaps you can relate. She watched as her husband had children with his other wife, Peninnah, but Hannah was left barren. And Peninnah's gloating over the fact didn't help. Hannah's heart grieved a life without children of her own. She approached God with tears and prayers.

In her deep anguish Hannah prayed to the Lord, weeping bitterly. And she made a vow, saying, "Lord Almighty, if you will only look on your servant's misery and remember me, and not forget your servant but give her a son, then I will give him to the Lord for all the days of his life, and no razor will ever be used on his head."
1 Samuel 1:10-11.

We are a little removed from the time period and Jewish culture, so we may not immediately grasp the significance of an unshaved head. God had set aside rules for a special group of men and women called Nazirites who would fully dedicate themselves to the Lord. Hannah pleaded with God to give her a son. If He did, she vowed to send him to grow up as a Nazirite. This vow was a tremendous sacrifice for a mother because it shortened the amount of time he would live under her roof.

Speak to the people of Israel and say to them, 'When either a man or a woman makes a special vow, the vow of a Nazirite, to separate himself to the LORD, he shall separate himself from wine and strong drink.... All the days of his separation, no razor shall touch his head. Until the time is completed for which he separates himself to the LORD, he shall be holy. He shall let the locks of hair of his head grow long.'
Numbers 6:2, 5 ESV

Note that verse 2 says "separation TO the Lord" not "FROM the Lord. This means that the child would serve the Lord as a Nazirite for his entire life. After Hannah poured out her heart to God, the anxiety lifted from her heart. The next morning, she worshipped God with renewed faith, no longer bitter or anguished. And God heard her prayer.

> *So in the course of time Hannah became pregnant and gave birth to a son. She named him Samuel, saying, "Because I asked the LORD for him."*
> 1 Samuel 1:20

The name Samuel means "heard by God" because God has listened to her despair and answered her prayers. After Samuel was weaned (tradition tells us that would have been when he was about three years old), Hannah took him to the tabernacle in Shiloh as she had promised God. She brought along with her a bull to sacrifice and money to tithe. She presented this child she'd longed for to the priests and gave her son over to the Lord—another mother on the bank of the Nile.

> *"I prayed for this child, and the Lord has granted me what I asked of him. So now I give him to the Lord. For his whole life he will be given over to the Lord." And he worshiped the Lord there.*
> 1 Samuel 1:27-28.

A Child of God

Mary, just like Hannah, knew that the child she was raising belonged to the Lord. She had to completely surrender control to Him and know that one day Jesus would be separated to the Lord.

This is not unlike our role as Christian mothers. While we are not handing our toddlers off to priests in synagogues, we are called to release our parenting to Him. We can trust Him with the hard things and seek Him for guidance as we raise these children of His.

For me, the potty-training years were...challenging. Let's just say, they weren't my finest hour—or the kids'. Never before had I felt like a bigger failure.

I could write a book on how *not* to potty train because I made all the mistakes while the kids made all the accidents. For the sake of their adolescent pride, I won't go into the details here, but oh, do I have stories.

It was not until I surrendered potty training (yes, potty training) to the Lord, that I was given peace about the process. Then, I was better able to train my child with grace (for both of us) without feeling like a failure. Like I said, we can trust Him with the hard stuff—even if it's stinky.

God charged Mary with the role of raising Jesus until the time came for Him to get to work and begin His ministry. Our Lord, Christ, Savior, the Messiah, King of kings, the Word of God...

His entrance into earth was stripped of power and prestige. He took the form of a baby that grew for nine months within a mother's womb. *The Word became flesh.* For years, He was dependent on the service of His mother, Mary, to take care of His every need.

> *On coming to the house, they saw the child with his mother Mary, and they bowed down and worshiped him.*
> Matthew 2:11

In the book of Matthew, we see that Jesus was worshipped by the Magi as Mary cradled Him in her arms. From here on out, each time baby Jesus is mentioned in conjunction with Mary, He is listed first and is followed by "with His mother." This distinction was made from Jesus' birth until the time He was old enough to take on the role God had planned for Him.

Mary nursed Jesus. Cracked nipples, clogged ducts, midnight feedings—she was not exempt from the toll giving birth and nursing takes on our bodies. Jesus had to learn how to roll over, sit up, crawl, talk, walk, and so on, just like the rest of us.

Did He ever catch a cold? What was His first word? Did He topple over when He took His first steps? Mary witnessed the same milestones we experience with our own children, but her son had God's Y chromosome.

Jesus' first milestone was recorded in Luke—one I captured with each of my kids at the hospital: the first visitors. The shepherds rushed to meet the Messiah after the angel of the Lord announced

His arrival. These men gushed over the child and the holy moment they experienced in the field. Word spread about this miracle, and as it did, a mama's heart melted.

But Mary treasured up all these things and pondered them in her heart.
Luke 2:19

Just like any mother, Mary loved hearing the amazing things people were saying about her child. When someone tells me my child is smart or talented or special in any way, I beam with pride. Of course, I am one hundred percent biased and already know how special my children are. Hearing it from others confirms that I may actually be doing this parenting thing right.

I treasure such things in my heart. For Mary, these were reminders of God's anointing on her child.

As was customary for Jewish parents, Jesus was circumcised on his eighth day. They took Him to Jerusalem to be consecrated to the Lord, their firstborn son. Mary and Joseph offered a sacrifice in the temple as per God's laws as mentioned in Exodus and Leviticus.

While there, a man named Simeon, persuaded by the Holy Spirit (Luke 2:25-35), and a prophetess named Anna (Luke 2:36-38) praised God and spoke of the salvation and redemption that were going to be brought to Israelites and Gentiles through Jesus.

The child's father and mother marveled at what was said about him.

Luke 2:33

Awe surged through Mary all over again. She had a front-row seat—and a supporting role—to witness the most incredible period in history and God's greatest blessing to the world. Whenever I take the time to let the enormity of God's majesty sink in, I feel it, too. Awe.

Mary and Joseph faced many difficult choices when they became parents. King Herod heard the rumor about the birth of the king of the Jews. The Magi spilled the beans. The king was set on killing all the baby boys knowing one of them would threaten his throne. An angel of the Lord prompted Joseph to escape with Mary and Jesus to Egypt until after Herod's death. God then guided them back home to Nazareth—the very place where the angel of God first appeared to Mary many years before. Full circle.

Train Up a Child

Mary gave birth and held Jesus in her arms—the Son of God. She fed Him, burped Him, changed His diapers, taught Him about His Father, caught Him when He stumbled as He took His first tentative steps, and bathed Him ever so gently. God humbly placed Himself under the care of a *mother*.

He has designed us for that same role. Mary watched her Son grow up to fill the role God had designed for Him. It is our hope that our own children will grow up and fill the role God designed specifically for them, too.

The time came for Jesus to begin His ministry on earth. He was thirty. John baptized Him in the Jordan River.

I saw the Holy Spirit descending like a dove from heaven and resting upon him. I didn't know he was the one, but when God sent me to baptize with water, he told me, "The man on whom you see the Spirit come down and remain is he who will baptize with the Holy Spirit." I have seen and I testify that this is the Son of God.

John 1:32-34

With the baptism, this child Mary raised was fully consecrated to fulfill His duty as the Messiah, the Christ. Mary always knew the day would come. She understood her own role and that of her Son. Oh, that we will be so blessed to see our children rise up to follow Him.

Take a moment to prayerfully consider the role God has entrusted to you. We are stewards of the next generation. A child is precious in His eyes and He desires a relationship with him or her. While we may worry about them, our children are in His hands and never out of His sight. As we parent, our job is to guide them to

Him, teach them His ways, and intercede for them in prayer. Pray this prayer over each of your children, placing their names in the blank below.

Heavenly Father, I am so thankful that you have entrusted me with the role of motherhood. You strengthen and equip me. I desire to follow Your good and perfect will as I raise _____. May he/she come to know You. Lord, I pray _____ will love and follow You all the days of his/her life. Amen.

FAITH AT HOME

FRUIT OF THE SPIRIT

Using sticker labels (or paper strips and tape), write sins (lying, yelling, disobeying, hitting, arguing, talking back, hurting someone, bullying, etc.) Make nine paper signs, one with each fruit of the Spirit (love, joy, peace, patience, kindness, goodness, faithfulness, gentleness, self-control).

Punch holes at the top two corners and tie yarn around each sign. Make one more sign and draw a cross on it. Stick the labels of sin all over your body.

Have the kids take them off one by one and stick them to the cross. When all the labels are removed, let the kids place each of the fruits of the Spirit around your neck. Lead the children in a parade march. Have them try to keep in step with you: right foot, left foot, right foot, left foot.

Repeat the activity as each of your kids wear the stickers, then the signs, then lead the parade.

But the fruit of the Spirit is love, joy, peace, forbearance, kindness, goodness, faithfulness, gentleness and self-control. Against such things there is no law. Those who belong to Christ Jesus have crucified the flesh with its passions and desires. Since we live by the Spirit, let us keep in step with the Spirit.

Galatians 5:22-26

CHAPTER 19

LOST & FOUND

My water broke. It gushed much like it does in the movies, yet it took me a minute to convince myself that I hadn't simply had an accident. It was still ten days before my due date. My husband was at work, and, for whatever reason, I had driven him there that day. I called to let him know I was 83 percent certain my water broke and that my mom and I would pick him up on the way to the hospital.

I was the calm one of the bunch. I took a nice, relaxing shower. I stood in front of my closet for what felt like ages to decide what outfit I would wear to the hospital. It seemed like an important decision at the time. I packed and repacked my hospital bag. I went to the bathroom a few more times, put on a little makeup, dried my hair, and changed clothes again because, yup, that definitely wasn't pee. Maybe. Apparently, contractions hadn't started because I felt like I was floating on a cloud. I was about to be a *mom*.

By the time we pulled up at my husband's office, he had nearly worn a path in the parking lot from pacing back and forth for hours. This was before texting was a thing and when people counted minutes on their phones. I hadn't told him it would take me a while to pick out my pre-hospital gown outfit.

Thirteen hours later, I held my baby in my arms. Thirteen years later, James greeted me with, "Happy Mom Anniversary." *Happy Birthday, son.*

Safe in God's House

When I was three years old, my parents lost me in a record store. Rather, I hid from them. The manager immediately put the store on lockdown to look for me, but I was playing hide and seek inside the storage cabinets. In my mind, there was nothing wrong with it.

Why should they worry? I was just playing a game. A game *they* taught me. But from their perspective, anything could have happened to me. As a parent, I get it now. I'm no longer the calm, soon-to-be-mom as my husband paced in the parking lot. We've both worn out a path on this crazy adventure called parenthood.

Mary and Joseph had a similar experience with Jesus. As crowds of people returned home from the festival in Jerusalem, surely Jesus was among them. After a day of travel, Mary and Joseph realized He was nowhere to be found. Hurrying back to Jerusalem, they found him three days later in the temple sitting among the teachers, asking and answering questions.

His mother said to him, "Son, why have you treated us like this? Your father and I have been anxiously searching for you."
Luke 2:48

Oh, if there is any moment throughout these stories of the mothers in the Bible that I can relate to most, it is this one. Several years ago, I took my children to a swimming party. They are all great swimmers, but still, I made sure I had a clear line of sight to the pool.

Mid-conversation with my friends, I looked up and only counted two Hiltys. I panicked as my eyes searched for her pink swimsuit among a pool full of boys. My littlest one was on the side of the house, out of my eyesight.

I think I said the same words Mary did when I found her, but maybe with more eyebrow action, a raised voice, and some finger-wagging.

"Why were you searching for me?" he asked. "Didn't you know I had to be in my Father's house?"
Luke 2:49

Mary, who had had the opportunity to speak to God's angel face to face and was the first to know that her child was *the* Son of God, still worried. It is ingrained in us as mothers to be concerned about our children.

> *But they did not understand what he was saying to them.*
> Luke 2:50

We easily forget that God is our shelter and refuge. There's safety inside His house. When we want to freak out about our circumstances are when we most need to seek Him.

Even when things don't work out the way we planned, even when our children are disobedient, sick, or heartbroken, or when we walk through grief, He is a safe haven.

Come to Jesus

Jesus, His disciples, and Mary had a wedding to attend. Jewish feasts and celebrations, such as weddings, were culturally significant in Old Testament times and beyond.

The wedding celebration didn't just last for a few hours, but for several days, sometimes even a week. The hosts were expected to provide food and wine throughout the course of the event or risk public embarrassment.

Mary must have played an important role in the wedding preparations and was close to the bride or groom's family. When she realized the wine ran out, instead of gossiping about the situation, she ran to Jesus for help.

"Woman, why do you involve me?" Jesus replied, "My hour has not yet come."
John 2:4

Side note: To be clear, Jesus was not disrespecting His mother. Just as in John 19:26, when Jesus addresses Mary as "Woman," it is a term of affection, endearment. The NLT Bible translation uses the phrase "Dear woman..." to emphasize Jesus' kindness and respect in the way He spoke to His mother.

Though it truly was not yet time for Jesus to reveal Himself as the Son of God, this was credited as His first miracle. It was an act of friendship toward the bride and groom, and a generous response to His mother's request.

Mary came to Jesus for something we might consider trivial, yet He made it happen. The bride and groom would not have seen it as trivial—anything that goes wrong on a wedding day feels larger than life—but it was not an issue of eternal significance. Jesus was concerned not only with the big things, but also the small matters of enjoyment.

We are invited to come to Jesus for His help with life's little pleasures. We can ask Him for guidance about saving money for vacation, for guests to attend your child's birthday party, or for the opportunity to have a girls' night with friends. I've prayed for all three of those. Jesus knows and cares about even the smallest desires of our hearts, and if they fall inside His will, He will make them happen. He just wants us to come to Him.

At the height of Jesus' ministry, He was followed by crowds of thousands. I imagine it was difficult to get a quiet moment with Him. Mary and Jesus' brothers braved the crowd one day to speak to Jesus.

> *He replied to him, "Who is my mother, and who are my brothers?" Pointing to his disciples, he said, "Here are my mother and my brothers. For whoever does the will of my Father in heaven is my brother and sister and mother."*
> Matthew 12:48-50

If my son had said that to me, it would hurt this mama's heart. But read these verses again. Jesus was not speaking to Mary, nor was he denouncing his biological family. Instead, He was announcing to the crowd the significance of living a life of following Him.

He was speaking of a brotherhood of the heart—the roots of Christianity. He knew his family intimately and invited the crowd into that kind of relationship with Him.

His ministry was to bring people to His Father. Mary's role had shifted from taking care of Jesus to becoming a follower of Jesus.

But I imagine she was beaming from the crowd as she watched her Son teach and lead people to God.

My kids are still young, but I know the time will fly by before they leave our nest. It's hard for parents to let go. I'm in the "sweet spot" right now. They can make their own breakfast, wash dishes, clean their rooms, and ride bikes down the street without me by their side.

I'm glad to have laundry helpers—a huge perk. Other things are harder to let go. I have to resist packing their loveys for a car ride. I want them to sit in my lap while we watch a movie. I want to hold their hands forever.

They still come to me when they are having a hard day, but soon they may not want me to scratch their backs and kiss their foreheads. A shift is happening on our parenting journey and I'm not sure a mother is ever truly ready for it.

I'm wearing trenches in my prayer walks as they gain independence.

Her Son's Last Breath

Mary, mother of our Lord and Savior Jesus Christ, witnessed her Son's first breath, heard Him cry as He sucked in the night air—and His last as He cried out to His Father. The loss of her child was not felt any less because He was the Messiah.

She lost her Son. Her baby.

She knew Him better than anyone—his birthmarks, His dimples, the texture of His hair. He had some of her features.

He was betrayed by His people, mocked, and nailed to a cross to suffer excruciating pain. A Son crucified as a mother watched on.

Many women were there, watching from a distance. They had followed Jesus from Galilee to care for his needs.
Matthew 27:55

Standing near the cross were Jesus' mother, and his mother's sister, Mary...and Mary Magdalene. When Jesus saw his mother standing there beside the disciple he loved, he said to her, "Dear woman, here is your son." And he said to this disciple, "Here is your mother." And from then on this disciple took her into his home.
John 19:25-27 NLT

Jesus' parting words to His mother, the woman who devoted her life to caring for her children, are recorded here. Jesus made sure His mother was left in good hands and entrusted her to the disciple John.

Dear woman... (John 19:26 NLT) as He so affectionately called her.

The cross wasn't the end—it was only the beginning. His life on earth began in His mother's womb and ended triumphantly as He ascended into heaven. This time His mom knew He wasn't lost. He was safe in His Father's house.

After her Son left this earth, His disciples returned to Jerusalem:

They all joined together constantly in prayer, along with the women and Mary the mother of Jesus...
Acts 1:14

We have the beautiful and blessed opportunity to sit at His feet in prayer as He sits on the throne. *Come to Jesus.* It's an open invitation.

Whether it's in the middle of a celebration, or at the cross, no reason is too little or too big. Seek His face in all circumstances.

When He asks, "How was your day?" don't just answer, "Fine," like our kids do after a long day at school. Tell Him *all* the things, big and small. If it helps to write it out, say it out loud, sing it to Him, paint a picture, do an interpretive dance, whatever it is—He gave you those gifts, so use them to speak to Him. Spend time today doing just that at His feet.

FAITH AT HOME

LOST SHEEP HIDE & SEEK

First, establish safe parameters for hiding spaces (e.g., stay inside, don't climb the furniture, etc.). The children are the hiders and you are the seeker.

When you find your child, wrap him or her up in a giant hug and lavish praises on him/her. Tell the Parable of the Lost Sheep in Luke 15:1-7 and discuss how Jesus loves each one of His children.

> *Then he calls his friends and neighbors together and says, "Rejoice with me; I have found my lost sheep."*
> Luke 15:6

Variation: LOST COIN HIDE AND SEEK. Hide a dime in a room. Turn off the lights. Give the kids flashlights to search high and low for the dime. Tell the Parable of the Lost Coin in Luke 15:8-10 and discuss how Jesus is the light and He is in constant pursuit of His children.

And when she finds it, she calls her friends and neighbors together and says, "Rejoice with me; I have found my lost coin." Luke 15:9

CHAPTER 20

HER CHILDREN ARISE

I was a better mom before I had kids.

My child would use manners. My child wouldn't throw tantrums. My child would know how to read before kindergarten. My child would obey the first time.

Oh, how little credit I gave to children who have their own minds and personalities. And how little credit I gave to moms who were doing an amazing job despite the challenges of motherhood. I was so naive.

These mothers in the Bible set the standard for faith, humility, grace, obedience, love, respect, and servanthood. And yet, more often I use my ther-*mom*-eter to gauge if I'm "mom enough" by the world's standards.

I thought when I became a mom, I'd gain innate caregiver instincts, but I'm a terrible nurse and a sympathetic vomiter. I can't for the life of me keep up with housework. We eat pizza three nights a week and tacos the other four. I often have a short temper, crave alone time, and cringe when I hear my name on repeat. I compare myself too often to perfection and fall oh so short.

But where did my idea of the perfect mom come from? It came from the world. From social media. From the latest trend. From curated content. From filters.

And the funny thing is, there are so many differing opinions about how to raise our kids that we can't even agree on what a perfect mom looks like. We want to be Super Mom, but she is a figment of our imagination, created from pride, and with her priorities out of whack. What kind of mom does God want us to be?

Blessed Mothers

When Elizabeth heard Mary's greeting, the baby leaped in her womb, and Elizabeth was filled with the Holy Spirit. In a loud voice she exclaimed: "Blessed are you among women, and blessed is the child you will bear! But why am I so favored, that the mother of my Lord should come to me? As soon as the sound of your greeting reached my ears, the baby in my womb leaped for joy. Blessed is she who has believed that what the Lord has said to her will be accomplished."

Luke 1:41-45

When Mary visited her cousin, Elizabeth recognized right away that God was at work in both of them. God was using those women to raise two men who would change the world. The idea of what God would accomplish through them blessed them.

Three decades later, when Jesus was teaching, a woman in the crowd declared, "*Blessed is the mother who gave you birth and nursed you*" (Luke 11:27). Though He loved His mama, Jesus did not want to imply that Mary was #blessed simply by giving birth to Him. Blessedness is the eternal outcome of a relationship with God.

He replied, "Blessed rather are those who hear the word of God and obey it."
Luke 11:28

Mary fit that definition. Jesus was fully aware that Mary's blessedness came because of her obedience to God. He wanted to show the masses gathered around Him that they, too, could share in God's blessings simply by obeying His Father.

His mother had God's favor because of her willingness to say, "I *am your servant.*" God already knew the mother Mary would become. Her heart was known to Him. Jesus witnessed firsthand her strength and the sacrifice of her obedience.

Mary was the chosen mother, the prophesied virgin, who for nine months carried and gave birth to the Son of God. She was the first person to know that the Messiah had finally come to deliver mercy, healing, and salvation.

She was the only person to witness Jesus Christ on the day of His birth and the day of His death—from lying in a manger to hanging on a wooden cross. Mary heard His first breath and His last when he cried out, *"It is finished."* (John 19:30).

And generations later we look upon her and admire her humility, her grace, her servanthood, and her motherhood. She was special in the eyes of God and of His Son because she was a mother—but she was blessed because she loved God.

Her Son indeed did arise, and she is called for all eternity *blessed.* Mary's service to the Lord set things in motion to bring salvation to all people. She set an example for our obedience to the Lord as we raise children of our own.

In Matthew 5, Jesus began His Sermon on the Mount by listing the beatitudes which had a simple formula: who is blessed, followed by how God blesses them.

Blessed are the poor in spirit, for theirs is the kingdom of heaven.
Blessed are those who mourn, for they will be comforted.
Blessed are the meek, for they will inherit the earth.
Blessed are those who hunger and thirst for righteousness, for they will be filled.
Blessed are the merciful, for they will be shown mercy.
Blessed are the pure in heart, for they will see God.
Blessed are the peacemakers, for they will be called sons of God.

Blessed are those who are persecuted because of righteousness, for theirs is the kingdom of heaven.
Matthew 5:3-10

There is no "blessed are the mothers, for God has given them children." Perhaps we have subdued the idea of being blessed by hashtagging our good moments and happiness here on earth (*#blessed*). Instead, it is the reciprocity of us being obedient to God and God giving us access to Him. Blessedness is bigger than motherhood.

Her children arise and call her blessed.
Proverbs 31:28

We pray our children will gain an understanding of what it means to have a mother on her knees before the Lord. And on that day, when they rise up to be children of God, a host of angels will gather to rejoice and worship Him. Their eyes will be opened to see blessings pour out from a loving God to those of us who surrender their lives to Him.

If we keep Christ at the center of our hearts and homes, our kids will see God's goodness through us.

It is our faith in Him that guides us through our parenting journeys. We pray and trust our kids will realize that what we do for them through the work of our hands, the love poured out from our hearts, and spiritually through prayer has had an eternal impact on their lives. Hopefully, they will one day arise to know God and know that through our obedience to Him and by God's grace, we are indeed blessed.

FAITH AT HOME

SHARE YOUR TESTIMONY

Share your testimony with your kids. Use age-appropriate language and leave out details that you aren't comfortable sharing just yet. How did you come to know Jesus? Talk about what He means to you. If your kids have already put their faith in Christ, encourage your kids to do the same. Have them practice sharing their testimonies with their stuffed animals. Have them call family members to share their faith as well.

> *If you declare with your mouth, "Jesus is Lord," and believe in your heart that God raised him from the dead, you will be saved.*
> Romans 10:9

AFTERWORD

The mothers in the Bible were heroes of *faith*. Though they had many moments that were not Pinterest-worthy, these women chose faith over fear. Their walks were far from perfect, but they chose God's Word over the world. These are the mothers we can look up to:

Jochebed—Jehovah is her glory. God's plan for our children is out of our hands. Likely, He'll surprise us with something better than we could imagine. Take comfort and trust in God's faithfulness. That Nile River is pretty big, but our God is bigger.

Hagar. God placed the well at her feet. When we feel depleted, God brings the well to us and places it before us. Sometimes we're in a tough spot for a reason we can't see yet. These times help us to build a relationship with God and strengthen us. We are in a place that will ultimately put us in a position that will bring glory to God. We have to have faith to trust God where He has us and we'll find Him there.

The Shunammite Woman. Step by step she chose to weep forward. She teaches us to go to God first about everything, seek Him, grab His feet, and pour our hearts out to Him. Her fierce sprint toward God and her incredible faith paints a beautiful picture of how we can intercede in prayer for the lives of our children.

Tamar. Her obedience yielded generations of obedience. Tamar had a tough decision to make and fought to keep her place among God's people. She put herself at risk and was smart about it. We need her wisdom because people are out to discredit us. They want to point out our flaws. Sometimes it's our own spiritual brothers and sisters who do so. We have to know God and what He desires of us to be able to stand our ground and be witnesses of His testimony.

Rahab. She lived the rest of her life among God's people. There will be times when following God means going against the world. We may even shut out people—put boundaries up to distance ourselves from people who are trying to tear down the walls around us. We can still love and pour into people who do not know Christ. But, if those people are causing us to fall away from God, we need to walk away from that community and build relationships with other believers.

Ruth. Her sacrificial love led her straight into the arms of God. She was free to remarry, stay in her home country, and build a dream life there, yet she decided to follow Naomi. She inherited much more than property from her mother-in-law—and left a legacy of faith and love. We carry on that same legacy and our greatest purpose is to pass it down from generation to generation.

Bathsheba. She went on a journey from separation to restoration. She walked through sin alongside her husband and it brought heartbreak and turmoil to her family. But then, there was a revival and redemption that can only be from God. As we live out our faith, our lives are transformed. Our roles shift as our children grow, but they continue to be witnesses to God's role in our lives.

Mary. She held Jesus. The Christ. The Messiah. Our Savior. She swaddled, swooned, felt His heart beat against hers, smelled Him, smiled at His little baby coos, wiped His tears, held His hand, and washed His feet. God humbly placed Himself under the care of a mother and into her arms. She was blessed because she served Him.

These women didn't possess special qualities that we do not already have knit inside of us. They found their strength and their direction in God. Their faith carried them, their faith exuded from them, and their faith poured into their children, and their children's children, for generations upon generations.

We are blessed with the opportunity to glorify God, like the mothers in the Bible who came long before us, through our own stories of faith. It's never too late to grow in our faith. Your story—and God's—will continue through your children and your generations to come. But first, it's time for you to arise and continue on your faith journey. May God bless you and keep you always.

Father God, may I always trust Your word and seek Your face. As I desire to live in You, God, may I surrender my will and follow You every step of the way. May I bring glory to Your kingdom as I live out my faith and serve You. And Father, may that faith be passed down from generation to generation. Let my children arise as children of God, seeking salvation in Your Son. It is through Christ's name, who arose from Mary's womb and from the grave, that I am blessed to pray. Amen.

ACKNOWLEDGMENTS

In 2014, MOMentum, a Bible study group for moms was born with the amazing support from my church leaders. In that first group of 15 women, I taught lessons on Jochebed, Hagar, the Shunammite woman, and Bathsheba. That was my first glimpse into how the stories of biblical moms could shape our perspective of our roles as mothers.

I am grateful God preserved these mothers' stories in the Bible for women in our generation and beyond. These mothers in the Bible have taught me more about faith, godly character, and our role in raising the future generations—the important stuff—than any mom blog or parenting book ever could. I'm a better mom for it.

To all of the moms in MOMentum over the years: y'all are amazing moms and inspired the creation of this book. So thank you, thank you for all of your support, prayers, stories, laughter, tears, and potluck dishes (both store-bought and homemade—I loved it all).

God has gathered a small army of Christ-centered women (and a few good men) to embrace my writing journey as a ministry to draw others to Him. I am merely a vessel here as God planted seeds and ideas into my heart and transferred them to page. To God be the glory!

I'm grateful to my husband, Bo, for championing me, urging

me to keep going, praying over me, bouncing ideas around, reading and rereading each round of edits (you deserve a gold medal for most times someone other than the author has read this book), giving the best foot rubs, and taking on extra household duties on long writing days and nights. You're my favorite.

This book would not be what it is without my agent Cynthia Ruchti of Books and Such Literary Management. Your prayers, wisdom, time, ideas, and eagle-eye skills went far beyond your agenting duties. I have a four-page document called "Cynthia's Guide to Writing ~~Good~~ Well" that I've pieced together throughout the editing phases. You've challenged me with questions that begged me to delve deeper into scripture to find answers. That level of mentorship is priceless. You love big and your passion for good writing that is "hemmed in hope" (that's a Cynthia-ism) shows in everything you do. Thank you for taking a chance with me and this book. Thank you for making me a better writer. And thank you for your prayers! You mentioned that after this book is done "we will have stories to tell, you and I!" So many stories. We should write a book!

A huge thank you to our small group—especially Tory and Sean, Christa and Melvin, and Hillary and Derrick. Bo and I hit the jackpot to have y'all in our lives. Thank you for walking alongside me in the writing and the waiting. And to my dear friends Cady Cobb, Sara Richard, Rebecca Gregory, Erin Greneaux, Carol Mills, Amanda Andrepont, Erin Marsolf, and Megan Coleman who have all lent your ears and brains to this project and who have all consistently asked, "How's writing going?" That question alone means the world. Miriam Douglas, I'm forever grateful for your help on the first leg of this journey. Kay Hobbs—your prayers and check-ins have carried me through the last lap of this marathon and have held me accountable to finish strong.

I'm blessed to be a part of two amazing online communities of writers, many of whom I've had the privilege of meeting in person. My hope*writers (especially NWCF sleepover ladies) and Bookie Friends Forever (BFFs), I look up to y'all so much! Your words are Christ-centered, truth-filled, and powerful. I'm so thankful to be on this writing journey with each of you.

A special thanks to The Bayou Church for being an incredible church home to our family.

To my sister Crista Davis and sister-in-love Kristen Caruso—you two mean the world to me. You are both amazing mothers to the coolest nieces on the planet! I love you both so much. Gail and Jim—thank you for raising such an incredible, Christ-centered man who leads our family in faith, love, grace, and supernatural patience. You are amazing grandparents and are adored by all four of your grandkids—what a legacy of love!

To the future brides of James and John Leyson and to Lena Marie, Abigail Diane, Marley Kate, Mila Jane, Lyra Mae, Lucy Lynn, and Ruthny: if God calls you to the ministry of motherhood, may this book strengthen your walks with Jesus and continue to grow the seeds planted long ago. As our children, future daughters-in-love, nieces, and bonus daughter, my prayers for you will never cease.

And lastly, my mom, Victoria Dupré Dellinger, held many physical copies of rough drafts of this manuscript in her hands. It's hard that she isn't here to hold this final, published copy. She was my biggest cheerleader. There were many milestones in my life and my children's that we were all hoping she'd be here for, but we take comfort knowing she has an even better vantage point now living her best day ever for forever. Mom, you are blessed.

SOURCES

Bruner, Kurt and Olivia. "Session 1 – Faith: It Starts at Home." It
    Starts at Home. RightNow Media, 2012.

Constable, Dr. Thomas L. "Dr. Constable's Expository (Bible Study)
    Notes." Sonic Light. 2017. 14 Dec. 2014
    http://www.soniclight.com/constable/notes.htm

Merriam-Webster.com Dictionary, Merriam-Webster,
    https://www.merriam-webster.com/dictionary/stage. Accessed
    18 Jul. 2018.

Casey Hilty is a speaker, artist, author, worship leader, and elementary school teacher. Using storytelling, music, and visual art, she is passionate about taking mothers on a journey from apathy to awe to fall in love—or back in love—with God and His Word. Casey and her husband, Bo, have three hilarious and fun-loving, school-aged kids: James, John Leyson, and Lena. They serve as a host family to Ruthny, a soccer player from Haiti, who quickly became a bonus member of the family. The Hilty family is immersed in Cajun culture and lives on a tee-tiny farm in South Louisiana affectionately called #LenasBigFarm. You can find her on Instagram @caseyhilty and Facebook @caseyhilty1.

For more Faith@Home activities, scripture art, speaking topics, and more, visit www.caseyhilty.com.

MORE FROM CASEY HILTY

AUTHOR. SPEAKER. WORSHIP LEADER. ARTIST.

WWW.CASEYHILTY.COM

- Subscribe for access to free devotionals, Faith@Home activities, Bible reading plans, digital art downloads, encouragement, and more for you and the family.
- Discover ways Casey can serve you and your community through speaking, leading worship, or creating custom art for your event.
- Shop for scripture art, family faith resources, and a new family Christmas tradition: the Nativity Garland.

@ CASEYHILTY

@ CASEYHILTY1

Made in the USA
Las Vegas, NV
07 October 2023